ART FOR SALE

A Candid View of the Art Market

DIRK BOLL

ART FOR SALE

A Candid View of the Art Market

HATJE
CANTZ

For BSV

Contents

An Historical Overview

Art—its creation, presentation, and reception—is in the limelight. Attendance numbers at museums, galleries, art fairs, and auctions have swelled. As if in counterpoint to the increased attention, public debates have examined the societal value of the museum and its classic tasks of collecting, preserving, and researching art. Despite the prices paid for masterpieces, public sector budgets have shrunk and more than a few skeptics have questioned the value of cultural spectacles. Not only has the discourse on art taken on even more political controversy, the controversy itself has been duly echoed in the media, garnering art both more attention and more opprobrium.

Because art *is* for sale. Many observers perceive the commercial art market as an expanding system that is gradually gaining total control over the public reception of art, while at the same time setting aside the hegemony of museum or academic experts. Large art fairs and auctions serve as windows on these processes, simultaneously drawing attention to the changes in power relations within the market—namely, the relationship between two competing distribution systems: the gallery/art dealer and the art auction.

In other areas of the economy, the technological development of the Internet has brought about greater transparency, above all because the Internet makes it considerably easier to access information. The art market is also accelerating, leading to an increase in the number of events. As a system, however, the art market has always understood how to maintain control over the flow of information. This book begins with a description of the structures, participants, and parameters—or, in other words, a candid view of the art market.

At the same time, it is clear that, over the past ten years, the parameters and distribution of roles in the art market have undergone changes that have caused serious questions about the usual way of allotting functions. Originally, art auctions were primarily intermediaries and the main source of art for art dealers. As late as the nineteen-thirties, retail buyers were obviously in the minority at auctions.

For about thirty years now, auction houses have been rethinking their roles. The limited number of artworks available makes it difficult to employ modern planning methods of buying and selling. Since profits cannot be maximized by increasing the number of objects sold, the only alternative is to increase demand and achieve the concomitant rise in prices. In order to do this, however, more retail buyers must take part in auctions. More competition among bidders raises the price level; also, buyers acting on their own behalf are not obliged to secure a profit by reselling a work at a price in line with the market. So it is now clear that auction houses have begun the move from wholesale to retail.

In recent years this development has only strengthened; the competition between auction houses and art dealers, which has been going on since the mid-nineteen-eighties, can be described as a predatory competition. Meanwhile, more than half of all of the objects sold on the market are sold at auction. The 1990–91 and 2008–09 crises in the art market have exacerbated the situation. Large, financially sound auction houses in particular sought market niches that they could fill with their own goods or services. Art dealers already established in these niches realized that the foundation of their business was increasingly insecure.

Will the changes in parameters and fundamentals of the art market—along with the expansion of auction houses into sectors of the business formerly occupied by art dealers—drive dealers further into niche markets? This might turn out to be the case at the top echelons where the growing lack of items to sell will shut out other types of intermediaries altogether; on the other hand, at the level of inferior quality, where the average price is so low that auctions are not really a sensible business option, sales made through Internet platforms are tightening the competition to an extreme degree.

The Art Markets

The art market examined here deals with fine and applied arts. Between the artist (the producer of the commodity) and the buyer (the consumer) are the art market intermediaries. Commercial intermediaries that sell art as a commodity—meaning (gallery) dealers and auction houses—have their counterparts in content mediators. As far as the process of handing down cultural values and creating social identity is concerned, the museum is the mediator. As for the role that social discourse plays in defining art and culture, the intermediaries are the media, and art criticism and theory.

The art market can be divided into primary and secondary markets. The artist and his representative sell the artist's work on the primary market, while galleries, art dealers, or auction houses resell these commodities on the secondary market.

In past years and decades, the art market has not just changed a great deal overall, but the rate at which changes are taking place is constantly accelerating. There is no model, no analytical instrument, for making prognoses about the art market. The reason for this is that commerce and structures here are commonly perceived within the parameters of art, not economic parameters. It is not possible for any sort of economic analysis to depict the connection between the content of a work of art and its value. Unlike most other areas of commerce, there is not much reliable empirical data about total sales on the art market. There is little public information about art market sales figures; the subject is not specifically addressed by government statistics offices or by the European Union.

Hence, the only way to ascertain developments on the art market is to examine the indices and sales figures of individual firms. And here, in turn, only auction house sales figures can really provide any meaningful information, since dealer sales usually just encompass individual microtransactions and are, as a rule, not public information. Nevertheless, it is true that, in terms of sales figures alone, the art market is the smallest sector in the whole culture industry. The art market's share in the world's gross national product is around 0.15 percent; Karl Marx called it a "quantité négligeable." All the same, art is not necessarily a luxury commodity, but instead, art sales hold a key position in popularizing the arts in general. About sixty percent of all art sales in Europe cost less than four thousand euro, while forty percent of sales are made for less than two thousand euro.

There is another reason why prognoses for the art market are vague and not particularly meaningful: this market is, de facto, the sum of various micromarkets, each of which comes with its own set of rules. Of course, there are basic parameters that are valid for the contemporary art market, the porcelain market, the antique furniture market, and the print market—to name just a few. At the same time, each of these micromarkets is subject to unique influences and trends. Predicting developments in the art market—that is, the sum of these submarkets—is not, therefore, a precise science.

A Question of the Right Place

When discussing the art market and its role as intermediary, there is always the question of how to deal with the commonly held idea that every work of art belongs in a certain place, and that, in the best-case scenario, the market will take it there, while in the worst-case scenario, it withholds it.

Since the artist intends to achieve an effect with his work, the right showplace for it determines, to a great extent, the way that a work can reveal its effect and be perceived by viewers. It is also indisputable that, depending on where it is exhibited, a work of art takes on a different context, becomes a new benchmark, and thus is capable of founding a new tradition. However, it cannot be forgotten that modern criteria of law, nationalism, or national legacy are frequently applied to a past based on different foundations, a past in which national states or organized international law did not exist. In addition, we have to distinguish between the cultural and geographical uprooting of the work of art (balanced out by the founding of public museums) and removing a work of art from the reach of society—something that does not occur in the museum, but on the market.

Since the market is blind to the question of the right place, the debate is about the issue of how much of the market art can actually bear. The perspective of author Heiner Müller—who thought that the art market robs art of the tranquility that it needs in order to reveal its subversive power—was refuted, even before the rise of Modernism. Instead, the market is a place where art is liberated from religion and from the authoritarian homage of the academy and museum. Today, saving art from the art market no longer simply means taking away its material foundation, but rather, it means demanding too little from it, in terms of intellect—even though, for a long time, it rose often enough to this challenge with zest. By contrast, the market indisputably proves rather helpless when confronted with old art, and that justifies state regulatory intervention as a corrective to the "blind" market, in order to protect cultural heritage and promote an active art collecting policy.

A Short History of the Art Market

Beginnings

Ever since art has been made, there has been a market for it. Even as early as 1500 BCE, Egyptian art dealers took their wares to Crete. At shrines in ancient Greece, images of the gods were sold to believers. Artists themselves, however, did not rank very high in society; a creative artist was merely the tool of the gods, who communicated through him. As a rule, works of art were not private property, but instead took the form of ornamented temples and altars. There are no known incidents of private, secular art collecting.

Nevertheless, there were early, important "political" collectors: the kings of Pergamum and the Egyptian pharaohs gathered works of art—whether purchased, received as gifts, or looted—in collections and treasure chambers. Still, there were no private collectors until the rise of the ruling class in Rome. Works of art were considered spoils of war, and if only for this reason alone, they were displayed in order to make an impression and subsequently sold. However, because Greek art was particularly admired, a different practice of collecting soon developed outside the display of military success. By the Imperial era, at the latest, it was important for every educated, wealthy Roman to have his own art collection. In order to serve the demand, a limited art market soon evolved. There was a street known for its large numbers of galleries and art dealers, the Via Saepta Iulia. Dealing in art, however, was frequently just an ancillary business for merchants mainly engaged in other types of trade. Artists themselves were the primary sellers of art, offering their own works for sale.

The Early Modern Market

After the fall of the Roman Empire and the rise of the Christian Church, which became the authoritative determinant of culture in Europe, the production of art was so heavily influenced by the Church that it would be difficult to say that there was an art market. The close relationship between patron and artist did not actually require any sort of intermediary. It was not until conflicts over dogma arose that a broader spread of knowledge became necessary, and this brought with it a growing demand for pictorial works. Still, this demand was essentially met by merchants, who not only sold art objects, but also hired their own artists. At this time, the professional artist came into being and gradually separated himself from Church patrons and guild regulations; his burgeoning self-confidence is honored in the writings of Albrecht Dürer and Leonardo da Vinci.

Art dealers do not reappear in the annals of history until the Renaissance. In Italy, from the late fifteenth century into the sixteenth, the aristocracy's passion for collecting was served by a network of agents and art dealers. During this period, auctions were increasingly regulated by the state—most heavily in France, owing to an edict issued by Henri II in 1552, which created a separate profession known as the *Huissiers-Priseurs* (bailiff-auctioneer), who were permitted to transfer property by auctioning it. This profession retained its special status in France until the harmonization of European Union laws abolished it in 2001.

A flourishing art market existed in the Netherlands in the sixteenth and early seventeenth centuries; the wealth created by Dutch trade could not be invested in real estate, because of the limited amount of land available. In addition, Calvinism, which prevailed in the country, favored a free art market, since the Calvinist ban on religious images eliminated the Church as a patron of the arts; hence, artists had to look for other avenues of profit. Consequently, this led to the establishment of trade relations (and not just in art) among all European countries, while artists who no longer worked exclusively on commission built up an "inventory" to sell. Works of art could be bought from studios, art dealers, and at an art market with more than one hundred stands set up in the Antwerp stock exchange, or at markets, auctions, and even lotteries.

This new kind of contextual and commercial brokering of art led to an artistic and economic boom in the Netherlands. For the first time, increasing demand from a large public determined the art market; it is said that, during this approximately hundred-and-fifty-year period, known as the Golden Age, around ten million paintings were produced. Additionally, the artists responded to this demand in a new way: instead of traditional and Biblical themes, production focused on popular genre pictures or landscapes. The Dutch art market was an exception in Europe and quickly acquired fame outside of political or economic boundaries, so that, for members of the English gentry, a visit to the studio of a Dutch artist became an established part of the so-called Grand Tour.

From the sixteenth century on, these tourists formed an essential group of buyers on the continental art market, at least until the Commonwealth, under Oliver Cromwell, arose in England. Puritan law forbade the importation of art from abroad. In contrast, when this law was lifted in 1680, the English aristocracy went on a spree. As the nation began its ascendancy in European trade, a great deal of money flowed into the country, while the Italian nobility became impoverished and had to sell. Last, but not least, the impressions gathered on a Grand Tour became the basis for individual collections, which soon became an indispensible part of a gentleman's social prestige. Due to the demands of the court in London—as well as the extreme increase in interest that arose somewhat later in Paris, especially among the wealthy bourgeoisie—these two capitals developed highly specialized, efficient art markets that outranked every other European cultural center.

The Auktionsverket was founded in 1674 in Stockholm, becoming the first of the international auction houses still surviving today, while Sotheby's, founded in London in 1744, is the second; Sotheby's, however, sold only books until well into the twentieth century. James Christie founded his company in 1766 in London; because he specialized in paintings and furniture, Christie's was the first real "art auction house" in the world. Christie was not only a charismatic auctioneer, but he was also acquainted with important public officials. His auction rooms in sophisticated Pall Mall quickly became a meeting place for the ruling elite after he sold the art collection of George Walpole, grandson of the British prime minister, to Catherine the Great of Russia, bypassing the "market" altogether. Christie was the first to recognize the potential in developing a loyal customer base by turning auctions into social events, which not only provided valuable entertainment, but also a place to enjoy art and have intellectual discussions. No longer was the auction house merely a place where money was exchanged for commodities, as they had been before. To this day, Christie's and Sotheby's still dominate the market, but this does not belie the fact that, throughout the centuries, there have been many competitors offering their services to clients. In the eighteenth century, there were about sixty other auction houses in London alone.

Early Expertise

During that period, ways of dealing in art altered greatly. Up until the mid-eighteenth century, paintings were generally attributed to famous painters, in order to boost the chances of selling them. Almost all of the Old Master paintings on the market were sold as works by Rembrandt, Veronese, Titian, et cetera. It was not until around 1740 that an art dealer in London, Arthur Pond, began noting his opinion on the back of each canvas he sold, as to whether or not the painting had actually been executed by the painter to whom it was ascribed. This practice gave him credibility, which turned out to be a great advantage, and countless others took up the practice (see p. 19 *The Modern*

Art Market). This development was in line with the spirit of the age, which witnessed the rise of lexicography, the encyclopedia, and literature. Many sales catalogues were produced, and these proved that their authors were experts who could vouch for the quality and authenticity of their wares.

At the same time, a French art dealer, Jean-Baptiste-Pierre Lebrun, began to think about the discovery of forgotten artists from earlier eras. He realized that, even though many of these artists were unknown, the quality of their pictures equaled that of famous paintings. This insight led to a permanent change in the role of the art dealer. Before, he was just a merchant, or, at best, a specialist in his field, but now, he was an art historian—and a speculator, since he could recognize a good painting and possibly purchase it inexpensively, and then, by applying his expertise, sell it at a higher price.

The French Revolution and the Napoleonic Wars considerably strengthened London's position as an art market, since it was here that aristocratic émigrés sold their only transportable property: works of art. Jewelry and precious stones were also in greater supply, so James Christie expanded his business to include this field. At the same time, numerous art dealerships were founded, where British collectors bought works of art rescued before the Revolution; these included Colnaghi and Sulley, dealers in Old Masters, and the Agnew Gallery, founded in 1817.

During this period, the growing economic power of the middle class contributed significantly to the development of the European art market, as did the founding of the first public museums and art associations in the early half of the nineteenth century. At last, the middle class was able to participate in the public collection and exhibition of art. Clubs specializing in history and antiquities also helped reinforce the bourgeois milieu's interest in private art and collecting. Beginning with the Great Exhibition at the Crystal Palace in London, answers were sought to aesthetic questions concerning such topics as the beaux arts or *arts utiles* décor of upper-middle-class interiors. Thus, the concept of the trade fair was born, and it has continued to the present day in the form of art and antiques fairs.

The Modern Art Market

Today's art market mainly has its roots in three almost contemporaneous developments: the economic rise of the United States after the Revolutionary War, the influence of the French Impressionists, and the reformation of British inheritance law in the second half of the nineteenth century.

In 1882 the passage of the Settled Land Act reformed inheritance law in Great Britain. As a consequence of industrialization and the flooding of the European market with cheap American wheat, the fortunes of British landowners were in decline. After bankruptcies began to mount, the inheritance laws were changed, making it possible for landowners to save their estates by selling their art treasures. Before 1882 estates were strictly settled, meaning that the head of the family did not actually own the land and chattels, while each member of the family was just a trustee of the family property. This was meant to hinder large estates from being sold off in sections. The Settled Land Act made it possible to sell individual portions of an estate in chancery court, in order to save the real estate. The treasures of the British nobility began to flow into London auction houses, shoring up their dominant position. At the same time, the United States' economy had progressed to the point where rich Americans could go to Europe to buy these goods. Besides the passage of this law, the early eighteen-eighties marked the public acknowledgment of French Impressionism. Prior to this, the Impressionists had been regarded as lunatics who painted under the influence of the delirium tremens and had declared war on beauty. But in 1881 Édouard Manet was named a Knight of the

Legion of Honor; in 1882 Paul Cézanne was allowed to exhibit for the first time at the Salon de l'Académie des Beaux-Arts in Paris, which had been the most important exhibition forum in the world since 1830, as well as a gathering place for contemporary art. In 1874, the annual group exhibition, which counterbalanced the official salon, featured only Impressionist works.

With the advent of Impressionism, the modern art market was born. Since most collectors rejected the Impressionists, the usual paths of distribution were closed to them, and they had to find other ways of selling their pictures. The rejection, however, meant that the artists were not dependent on the tastes of potential patrons, and, hence, they began to see themselves as autonomous masters. This approach also awakened a newfound respect for the art dealer, since he had access to genius and could open up the path to it by mediating and explaining it. In the early twentieth century Cubism arose and representationalism slowly began detaching from art—something that also strengthened the notion of the artistic genius, as well as that of the art dealer as intermediary. On one hand, the content of art became more complex, and on the other, it also became more difficult to understand and communicate.

One of the most successful dealers in contemporary art of the period was the Frenchman Paul Durand-Ruel. He was the first to sell the works of the French Impressionists, and, through his gallery in New York, he also introduced Impressionism to the American market. In Germany, it was publisher and dealer Paul Cassirer who recognized early on the quality of the French Impressionists' work. However, he also showed Max Liebermann and Ernst Barlach at his art salon in Berlin. In contrast to his European "centralist" colleagues abroad, he had only a small market, since sales took place in the various major cities of the German states (which were not officially unified until 1871), mainly in Munich, Düsseldorf, Hamburg, and

Berlin. This is the reason why the structure of the present-day German art market remains polycentric.

Around 1900, though, the center of contemporary art was Paris. Besides Durand-Ruel's establishment, there were only two other galleries showing contemporary works: Ambroise Vollard and Berthe Weill. In 1907 Daniel-Henry Kahnweiler, originally from Stuttgart, opened his gallery. Through his friendships with Pablo Picasso and Juan Gris, his gallery quickly became the center of an illustrious group of artists. As part of his collaborations with artists, he tried to secure them a steady income, so that they would be able to work independently.

The most successful dealer in Old Masters, however, was probably Joseph Duveen, the son of Jewish Dutch immigrants in Great Britain, who arrived in New York at the age of seventeen, in 1886. After a brief apprenticeship under his uncle, the art dealer Henry Duveen, Joseph opened a gallery in direct proximity to the Waldorf-Astoria Hotel, which was already the meeting spot for the city's wealthy elite. Duveen's business strategy entailed the purchase of complete collections. In this way, a client would be unable to calculate the dealer's wholesale price and, hence, the percentage he kept for himself. If he made purchases at public auctions, he did not shrink from paying record prices, since this practice brought him a reputation and also raised the value of the pieces he already had in his inventory. In addition, he was able to stir up enthusiasm among many industrialists for the idea of an American national foundation, which led incidentally to more collecting—the railroad, coal, steel, newspaper, automobile, oil, and bank millionaires regarded the acquisition of European masterpieces as an opportunity to assure the immortality of their names. Out of the original idea of a national foundation arose the National Gallery of Art in Washington, D.C., in 1937.

After Black Friday—October 25, 1929—the first great drop in the art market occurred. One result was that Sotheby's and Christie's considered a merger. For most of the art market, the recession lasted until the end of World War II. During the war, London's market profited from the fact that its main competitor, Paris, was occupied by the German army. The immigration of major artists affirmed New York's position as the new, international market for contemporary art. Many people gathered around one particular collector and gallery owner, a self-described "art addict" who brought the European and American avant-garde movements together: Peggy Guggenheim. Thanks to a large inheritance and the business experience she gained while operating a gallery in London (Guggenheim Jeune), she was able to open her gallery, Art of This Century, in 1942 in New York, where, until 1947, she exhibited works by artists such as Jackson Pollock, Max Ernst, George Grosz, Francis Picabia, Juan Gris, Robert Motherwell, Mark Rothko, Alexander Calder, and Willem de Kooning.

Postwar Developments

After the war, New York replaced Paris as the home of the avant-garde; many galleries came into being, including Leo Castelli's. From 1957 on, Castelli represented the majority of important contemporary artists, from Robert Rauschenberg, Jasper Johns, Frank Stella, and Cy Twombly, to Roy Lichtenstein. One reason he was popular among artists was his introduction of the "European system"—meaning that he paid each of his artists a monthly salary.

In Germany, after World War II, the contemporary art trade was confronted with the long and difficult process of starting all over again. Countless artists and dealers had emigrated between 1933 and 1945. Despite all this, the first galleries began opening in big cities in the nineteen-forties, followed by more in the fifties. Most were concentrated in the Rhineland, since that region was experiencing an economic boom. The most important auctions of the Modernist art declared "degenerate" by the Third Reich, however, took place at the Kunstkabinett in Stuttgart; there, between 1946 and 1962, Roman Norbert Ketterer—also the executor of Ernst Ludwig Kirchner's estate—auctioned German Expressionist works.

In order to reintroduce the public to Modern art after the "dark years" of National Socialism, the first documenta was held in Kassel in 1955. Over the years the documenta, held every five years, has turned into the largest exhibition of contemporary art in the world. For the art market, the exhibition was more than just a way to introduce Modern art to a wider audience. For the works, the documenta functioned as a first step on the way to the museum and had more than just a little influence on the prices of works by participating artists, however temporary.

An event that was to have a lasting effect on the art market was Sotheby's 1957 auction of the Weinberg Collection in London. It was the first time that an auction was professionally marketed as an event—even the Queen was invited, and she appeared at the preview, attended by a crowd of journalists. One year later the same firm auctioned eleven Impressionist paintings from the Goldschmidt Collection. It was also a premiere of sorts: the first evening sale in auction history. The bidders, clad in evening dress, were assisted by a catalogue of the works, the first such publication to contain color images.

Over the course of the nineteen-sixties, galleries established themselves as the place to acquire contemporary art, because of the generally high quality of shows as well as the great notice they attracted from an increasingly international audience. Due to their many connections to museums, which were backed by government-funded purchasing power, the galleries became a central focus for society. Openings were de rigueur for those who considered themselves part of the cosmopolitan elite.

From there, it was just a small step to the first contemporary art fair. Staged in Lausanne in 1965, the fair was organized by a group of gallery owners working together in a coordinated effort. Spurred on by their success, German participant Hein Stünke worked with Rudolf Zwirner to organize the first contemporary art fair in Germany in 1967, the Kunstmarkt Cologne. A "protest" exhibition was organized in 1968 in Düsseldorf in response to the criticism about the selection of artists for the Kunstmarkt Cologne. Under pressure from competing European fairs—ART Basel, founded in 1970, and FIAC, founded in Paris in 1973—the two German fairs merged. At first, they alternated exhibition sites, but finally, in 1989, it was decided to keep the exhibition in Cologne. Since then, it has been called Art Cologne.

Auction houses began selling contemporary art in the mid-seventies. This not only signaled a growing public and, hence, broader acceptance on the market, but it was also an indication that economic success could be obtained through more than just dealing in Old Masters. When the great houses began to take the sale of contemporary art seriously, it meant the end of the dealers' monopoly in this field.

Boom and Bust

At the start of the eighties, the economic upswing was not the only thing fueling the rise in art market sales figures. For the international art market, the growing "style consciousness" developing in the general population was critical. Collecting art and surrounding oneself with it in one's private life became part of a certain lifestyle, and an affinity for Modern art in particular was supposed to increase the collector's importance and garner him prominence and respect. At the same time, the avant-garde nature of contemporary art shifted to the foreground, because art was more metaphysically and philosophically charged, and declared a nucleus of real life. In order to be considered avant-garde, art had to be even more forceful than ever in its questioning of conventional tastes and established perceptions. This also led to a change in the status of art: previously, when one surrounded oneself with art as a sign of one's wealth, the art was not supposed to be too new, in accordance with the traditions of wealth. Now, however, Modern art not only became a status symbol due to its allegedly high price, but also—and primarily—because it indicated that the interested party or owner had the necessary education and intellectual curiosity required to come to grips with the work.

This development hit its apex in the late eighties, when art, lifestyle, and the autonomous work merged with popular advertising and consumer aesthetics. Art was talked about in the tabloids, and some artists became pop stars. Rising prices, in the meantime, motivated more owners to sell. In the decade between 1980 and 1990, the prices for Impressionist paintings increased around 940 percent, notwithstanding "Black Monday," the stock market crash of October 19, 1987. At first, the crash did not seem to affect the art market: the continuing rise in prices meant that art was a good alternative investment. That same year, the market was spurred on when a new world record was achieved: Christie's sold Vincent van Gogh's *Sunflowers* for 24.75 million pounds. That particular fall of the hammer triggered an avalanche of high-quality art auctions, which rapidly broke one world record after the next. Doubtless, the acme of this meteoric development was the week in May 1990 in which the Japanese paper manufacturer Ryoei Saito purchased Van Gogh's *Portrait of Dr. Gachet* at Christie's New York for 82.5 million dollars. At the time, this was the highest price ever paid for a work of art. Two days later, Saito bought Pierre-Auguste Renoir's *Bal au Moulin de la Galette* at Sotheby's for 78.1 million dollars. This was typical of the boom: it was sustained by Impressionist art and frequently paid for with Japanese money.

Shortly before these record-breaking sales, however, there were a number of signs the boom was losing momentum. Many individual factors, such as the stagnating Japanese economy, which heralded the financial crisis in Asia in the nineties; tax authorities' investigations of art acquisitions; and an increasing rate of unsold items at large auctions resulted in speculators withdrawing their money from the art market. Overnight, the market for Impressionist works collapsed. Panicked investors lost money in hasty sales, and for a long time, art was no longer considered a good speculative investment.

Cartels and Globalization

Anyone monopolizing a market is able to dictate terms and conditions to buyers. If there is no monopoly, but two competing companies dominate the market together, that is called a duopoly. It can turn into a monopoly if the two companies recognize that customers are dependent upon them, and then agree to act together to set prices.

According to United States law, secret agreements about collaborations and prices are considered a bar to free competition and are therefore illegal; the Sherman Antitrust Act of 1890 formulates the ban on monopolies in very general language. Because free competition is highly valued in American law, this open formulation is the basis for many individual regulations that can impose severe penalties on companies and employees that conspire to form monopolies.

On Christmas Eve, 1999, Christopher Davidge, then the CEO of Christie's, made a voluntary declaration in which he testified that the firm had, since 1993, been conspiring with Sotheby's, his company's most important and largest competitor, to set prices for services. Since, however, at the time, the two companies held ninety percent of the market share between them, this confession was relevant to cartel law. Thanks to Davidge's declaration, however, the company was able to protect itself and its employees from penalties, since the American justice system rewards the party that breaks the cartel and files charges.

As the investigation revealed, Davidge and Diana D. Brooks, Sotheby's CEO, met several times with the chairmen of the two companies, A. Alfred Taubman, of Sotheby's, and Sir Anthony Tennant, of Christie's. In 1992 they agreed to set the rate for sales commissions, and starting in 1995, they began agreeing upon the other types of fee structuring. Diana D. "Dede" Brooks and Alfred Taubman were indicted; during the trial, the former tried in vain to portray herself as an instrument manipulated by Taubman. In Taubman's version, however, Brooks had acted not only without his agreement, but also without his knowledge. The court did not accept his version either, but sentenced both companies to pay damages in the amount of 256 million dollars each. The main beneficiaries were customers who had sold something through one of the companies between 1993 and 2000, and those who had bought something between 1997 and 2000. For the two firms, the trial had broad consequences. Taubman and Brooks immediately resigned their positions in February 2000. Both companies announced the prompt restructuring of commission rates. The affair also gained a great deal of notoriety through the press.

Although dealers temporarily profited from the ill will toward the auction houses, the negative attitude vanished, surprisingly enough, after a few months, and things returned to normal. It took ten years of gradual price increases, but by the end of the nineties, prices in almost all of the market segments were close to where they had been during the boom. Consequently, the greater interest in contemporary art manifested by society as a whole quickly took on the role of "market driver" (see p. 83 *Painting*). The development that occurred in the eighties repeated itself in the two-thousands, as the globalization of art markets expanded demand. This went on until the international financial crisis of 2008, which put an end to soaring prices, especially in the contemporary art market.

However, the overall acceleration of the world economy has reduced the amount of time that passes between stock market crashes and price drops in the art market. In the case of the 2001 crisis, it took twelve months, but in 2008, only three months went by before the effects of the financial crisis were felt in the art market. Still, there are two significant differences between 1987–90 and 2008: for one, buyers in the twenty-first-century market are far more selective and quality conscious than buyers during the nineteen-eighties boom. Due to changes in society and the general expansion of interest in art, the market has many more customers. The large auction houses estimate that the number of active bidders was twenty times greater in 2008 than it was in 1998. Besides very strong growth in the total number of those active in the art market, new groups of buyers continually appeared, forming the basis for the boom between 2003 and 2008: Russian, Chinese, and Indian collectors followed those from the Gulf region and other Asian countries, such as Korea.

Since 2008, the international markets have largely recovered, thanks to low interest rates and weak currencies in the wake of the financial crisis. By 2010 prices at the high end of the market had mostly returned to their 2007 level. Owning art was once again seen as a way to counter inflation, or even as a sensible investment. The most obvious sign of this was that two world records were set in 2010: in February, Sotheby's in London sold a sculpture by Alberto Giacometti, *Walking Man* (1961), for 65 million pounds, a sum that was equal to 104.3 million dollars at the time, and thus slightly exceeded the price paid for the previous record holder, a work of Picasso's from his Pink Period. By May, however, the title of "most expensive work of art ever sold" again belonged to a Picasso, when Christie's in New York sold his painting *Nude, Green Leaves, and Bust* (1932) for 106.4 million dollars.

The Structure of the Art Market

Commercial Intermediaries

Between the two poles of the art market—the artist and the collector—there is a wide and often fluctuating world of individuals and institutions devoted to both the dissemination and interpretation of art. Although the art market itself is primarily a commercial intermediary, those who deal with the non-commercial contexts of art—what might be called "content-related intermediaries" (see p. 40 *Content-Related Intermediaries*)—also influence the participants in the system and, as a consequence, the market.

Art Dealers

Art dealers can be divided into three categories: art dealers, rare book dealers, and galleries. Around the globe, the differences among them are strong. The first two offer antiques and old art and books, while doing business in sales rooms, at fairs, and via the Internet. The term "gallery" encompasses private dealing in any sort of art, from the works of the Old Masters to multiples and posters. Traditionally speaking, however, a gallery is a firm that buys the work of contemporary artists, generally before they are picked up by museums. Here, the gallery does not just act as the middleman between the work of art and the buyer—it makes the artwork accessible to the public in both a concrete and an intellectual sense. As such, gallerists can be said to mediate the relationship between artist and buyer, often representing artists who have not yet developed a reputation. Even if it is not a precondition, a trusting relationship between the artist and the representative often ensues. After all, the primary market is the first chance that an artist has to gain some idea of the commercial value of his or her work. By carefully selecting the artists they wish to represent, gallerists also have the opportunity to create a program that will distinguish their particular company from the competition. Therefore, these primary galleries are sometimes referred to as "program galleries."

The gallery is the classic place for artists to have their initial shows and discussion forums; it is where artists expose their work to public critique for the first time. Ideally, the gallery takes on the job of introducing young and unknown artists to the market and thus has a hand in determining the artistic value of a work of art, as well as its market price, market strategy, and value to society. Hence, galleries occupy a key position in the art market, if not also in the process of determining the direction in which art as a whole will develop.

The optimal way for a gallery to make an artist known to the public is to sell his or her works, ideally to the most important museums and private collections. However, that path often entails difficult and expensive work, which is also entangled with high risk, since only a small minority of artists can actually flourish on the market at any given time—a gallery can only succeed by correctly balancing artists whose work sells sluggishly against those who reliably produce strong sales.

Yet another important function of the gallery is to encourage and educate new collectors. A gallery can advise collectors continuously over a longer period of time in a way that any auction house looking for new buyers cannot. Considering the fact that contemporary art increasingly needs explication, the influence of art dealers has grown steadily since the beginning of Modernism. It is obvious that art dealers are becoming progressively responsible for mediating art in society and culture.

The Auction

The auction is an organized way to sell goods to the public by gathering a potential group of buyers, either virtually or in person, at a particular time and under unified guidance. One characteristic of an auction is that the wares are sold at the highest price that can possibly be achieved, by accepting competing bids from interested bidders.

On the auction market, the two leaders are Christie's and Sotheby's; they are positioned opposite many other houses, which tend to be nationally based and—even for those that do operate internationally—have significantly fewer items to offer. Altogether, the two large international houses take up more than three quarters of the market. And while it would be difficult to claim a relationship of cause and effect, most of the new developments in this field of business are introduced first by one of these two houses, and their histories are exemplary of how the modern auction house developed. Their degree of fame is an important instrument on the supply side of this market, as well as something that conveys a sense of security to clients, since—due to their dominance of the market—these houses are watched more closely than others.

A Mix of Trade and Auction

One frequently occurring blend of both these businesses comes in the shape of the dealer who also acts as an auctioneer. This kind of combination, however, tends to form inadvertently. An art dealer tries to acquire more clients through a new channel—the auction—while at the same time, she purchases new items for her own dealership from clients who want to sell their objects. Or, an auctioneer buys something through his own auction and thus creates another channel for making a sale, namely by then acting as a dealership. The latter is problematic, since at that point the auction house is no longer a neutral intermediary hoping to achieve maximum profit. Instead, buying in its own auctions, it competes with other dealers who want to purchase items through the auction and are hoping to pay the lowest possible hammer price.

Procuring items for auctions, however, can also be the reason for this kind of double track: owners of smaller auction houses in the provinces, especially, where there are fewer potential clients than there are in the big cities, behave like dealers and buy objects, which they then turn around and sell in their own auctions. As a result, the true character of the acquisition remains hidden, and the auction house is no longer a neutral intermediary (see p. 125 *Competition for Supply*).

Yet another hybrid consists of a dealer and an auction house. One well-known case is that of the Villa Grisebach auction house—the most important house for prewar Modern art in Germany today. The "Villa," originally the house of architect Hans Grisebach on Fasanenstrasse in Berlin, was founded in 1986 by art dealer Bernd Schultz and four other colleagues. The dealers operate their galleries as well as an auction house.

However, if an auction house buys a share of a gallery in order to gain access to their client list and, above all, to have a discreet place to offer works not sold at auction, then this is an attempt to use the gallery as another sales conduit (see p. 171 *New Distribution Channels*).

Consultants, Experts, Detectives

Consultants play an important role in the art market. During the acquisition process or in carrying out individual projects, they provide support to collectors or museums with their knowledge of art history, tax law, or business. Consultants are particularly important to corporate collections. To the extent that a company regards its collection as a publicity tool and a way to motivate employees, the private preferences of individual managers are set aside in favor of expertise, which can often only be provided by a professional consultant.

Individual contracts define the field of duties performed by art consultants. A consultant is obligated to provide correct, complete information in a conscientious manner, and to investigate information provided by third parties. Representatives of this profession like to consider themselves objective, and—if they have no financial interest in a business—as neutral mediators. Other types are still rare; only very large private collections have permanent, salaried curators who are not dependent on their commissions. Inversely, galleries now have departments that offer consultation apart from their daily business, so that the boundaries between gallery deals and art consulting are becoming increasingly blurred. Artists who want to be engaged in the process of selling their own work also employ the services of art consultants.

In a few countries, consulting is carefully regulated. Independent art experts in Germany are certified by the Chamber of Industry and Commerce (or, in France, by the Auctioneers Council), and must be publicly appointed and sworn in. The job of these experts is to establish the authenticity and value of artworks, and to act as advisors for insurance purposes and in court. In order to be appointed, a consultant has to have a previous knowledge of art history, several years of professional experience in the art market, and be at least thirty years old. The institutions that appoint them publish lists of approved experts.

Architects and interior decorators also occupy important positions in the art market, since they advise their clients in matters revolving around interior décor. In cases when art and artisanal furnishings are bought simply to enhance a living environment, the advice of this group of professionals cannot be underestimated. In the United States, above all, wealthy clients might well order all of their furnishings, including works of art and antiques, from their interior decorators; in New York, up to eighty percent of antiques buyers are interior decorators.

Finally, banks and insurance companies are also offering art consulting as a service to their clients, since the acquisition of art generally affects the types of services offered by these companies (financing, investment advice, financial planning, and insurance). Services, however, can go far beyond the intersection of art acquisition and banking, and range from planning collections, acquiring works, estate planning, and appraisal, to founding and administering foundations. These services can be performed for an hourly rate, or on commission, depending on whether (in terms of proprietary law) structural consulting is done or only assistance with transactions is provided.

One last type of service provider should not go unmentioned here: the art detective. Should a collector be looking for a lost object, he is frequently dependent upon the help of a detective, for lack of other alternatives. An art detective will research the whereabouts of lost objects, or the proprietary rights to well-known (museum) pieces. These types of service providers can be hired by a previous owner or the museums affected, or else they can also work on their own initiative. As a rule, a detective will be paid by the party that hires him, generally at a fixed salary, with reimbursement of business expenses, and a bonus if the job is completed successfully—something like a finder's reward. The successful detective must negotiate this with the owner of the lost work of art; if he finds it, he might earn up to fifty percent of its value.

The Art Market and the Luxury Market

In the art market, the relatively small size of most businesses also diverts attention away from the fact that the large auction houses have, in the meantime, become part of international corporations. Integrating an art business into a corporation, such as a fashion group, can create synergy, since both are aiming at the same clientele.

To increase their rate of returns in particular, more and more firms have been trying since the mid-nineteen-nineties to position themselves "higher" on the market, in order to turn their products into premium products. After it was realized that an established brand is priceless in terms of marketing, a real hunt for brand names started in the luxury goods segment of the market. Here, it was all about elevating the position of the entire brand, or the "mother brand," in order to raise revenue.

In all kinds of markets, there is a difference among commodities whose quality is known and can be assessed during a purchase (so-called search goods, such as fruits and vegetables, for example), goods whose quality cannot be evaluated before the purchase, but must be experienced first (so-called experience goods, such as canned foods), and goods whose quality cannot really be evaluated even after purchasing them (so-called credence goods, such as the services of an attorney). A brand is one way to turn an experience good into a search good, because the brand's quality is reliable. This is often not enough when it comes to credence goods, since the consumer cannot evaluate the quality of the goods himself and must rely upon specialists. If a brand mainly consists of opinions and evaluations, then, in terms of experience goods, it is a medium particularly suited to the process of establishing identity and value. Here, the brand generates trust in the system—the system, whose performance is supposed to lead to the desired success, is trustworthy down to the last detail. This is the way that brands contribute to the success of banks, insurance companies, and international auction houses.

Alfred Taubman has to be regarded as one of the pioneers in this development. The inventor of the "shopping mall" added the crowning touch to his construction and real estate empire in 1983, when he acquired a majority interest in Sotheby's. For the entrepreneur, however, this move was seen more as a "door opener" to society, as it only linked his luxury real estate business with the name of the posh subsidiary, but not any other branch of his company. For tax reasons, Sotheby's became an American company and since then has been headquartered in New York.

Sotheby's is the prototype of an art market brand: traditional, prestigious, established in every way, yet still vibrant. The power of the Sotheby's brand can only be compared to that of Christie's—other old brand names on the art market, such as Knoedler, Wildenstein, or Colnaghi, are nowhere near as famous.

The Rivals: Pinault vs. Arnault

François Pinault was the first entrepreneur to use the brand name and the potential of an art market company as a strategic guide for his consortium. The French department store chain Printemps and the mail-order company Redoute comprised the core of his group of companies. Since both were positioned in the upper echelons of their respective markets, they produced reliable profits that financed the purchase of other companies.

Over a period of many years, the parent company, PinaultPrintemps-Redoute (PPR) expanded its portfolio of luxury retailers and manufacturers. Among Pinault's holdings are Parisian fashion label Yves Saint Laurent, American luggage maker Samsonite, the Château Latour winery, Gucci, Bottega Veneta, PUMA, watch manufacturer Girard Perregaux, and the fashion labels of Alexander McQueen and Stella McCartney.

Pinault was the first to realize that providers of luxury goods and services in various branches were frequently competing for the same customers—anyone with the money and taste to wear Saint Laurent would also very likely buy expensive shoes, or art. This led to his first acquisition on the art market: in 1998 he purchased Christie's, the largest art business in the world. The brand's tradition, image, and potential, as well as its many real estate holdings in St. James's and Kensington—popular and costly London locations—made the company an expensive acquisition: Pinault paid a total of 721 million pounds (around 1.2 billion dollars at the time).

Imitators soon began employing the same strategy. The most consistent is a former close friend of Pinault's, Bernard Arnault. He began his entrepreneurship with Louis Vuitton Moët Hennessy (LVMH). The consortium is named after Louis Vuitton (handbags and luggage), Moët & Chandon (Champagne), and Hennessy (cognac). Determinedly buying up one company after the next, from Dior to Veuve Cliquot, Arnault turned LVMH into the largest provider of luxury goods in the world.

The Battle for the Art Market

Both businessmen—Arnault and Pinault—like to portray themselves as art lovers and passionate collectors. Their rivalry is not exhausted in the battle for individual works of art. Arnault wanted to level the field between himself and Pinault by trying to take over Sotheby's. After this plan was blocked by Alfred Taubman, he concentrated on the number three company in the world, the London auction house of Phillips. However, since the Phillips brand name and the value of its real estate were not worth as much, the price paid—an estimated 80 to 100 million pounds, or 132 to 165 million dollars—was comparatively low.

Still, Arnault saw potential in Phillips, and thought it would be able to join the ranks of the largest companies at some point, especially when the two leading companies in the market violated American cartel law, which led to a brief, yet serious credibility crisis, especially in the United States (see p. 26 *Cartels and Globalization*). With the backing of LVMH millions, the company was immediately re-launched: new corporate identity, catalogue design, and massive replenishment of all of the marketing budgets, on one hand, and, on the other, all of the firm's departments were expanded.

Arnault also succeeded in hiring art dealers Simon de Pury and Daniella Luxembourg to run Phillips. De Pury had been the chairman of Sotheby's Europe for many years, until he and his colleague, Daniella Luxembourg, opened their own business in Geneva in 1997; at that time, de Pury was considered one of the world's best auctioneers. In 2001 the Geneva art dealership de Pury & Luxembourg merged with Phillips. Phillips focused on its expansion plans in the long-neglected New York; shortly after the takeover, it was speculated that, due to the huge importance of the American market, the auction house would move its headquarters there. This, however, did not occur until November 2001, when the London branch merged with Bonhams: Phillips would only see itself in the upper echelons of the market, and gave up its smaller departments (see p. 172 *The Battle for the Middle Market*). Simon de Pury had the desire and ambition to concentrate on the top market sector and had been talking about it ever since he joined Phillips. Ultimately, this was the same path taken by the two larger competitors, although they retained their smaller departments.

The main difference among the companies was that Pinault owned PPR and its affiliates, while Arnault, as the executive partner, had to look out for the interests of the other shareholders. One aspect of this situation is that the Pinault companies are not required to provide any information about the consortium's finances, which is not the case with the competing group. This became an important point with respect to the immense amounts of money LVMH had invested in Phillips. For Arnault, his passion for art and his rivalry with Pinault may have been sufficient reasons for him to invest money in one of the subsidiaries, without any expectation of short-term profits. If there is an obvious gap between the entire group's sales and profits, however, shareholders generally try to find out why.

Arnault's activities on the art market came to a surprisingly quick end. As the share prices of the LVMH Group dropped and Phillips sustained huge losses, Arnault gave in to the pressure from management and shareholder representatives in 2002 and agreed to reduce LVMH's holdings in Phillips. In December 2001 the price of LVMH stock plunged from a fifty-two-week high of 183.70 euro to 48.88 euro (at the time, 188 to 50 dollars, approximately). De Pury and Luxembourg became the major shareholders. In the last chapter of this story, Luxembourg sold her shares to de Pury in March 2004. Since then, the company has been known as Phillips, de Pury & Company. In 2007 de Pury managed to find new investors. By October 2008 Leonid Friedland and Leonid Strunin and their Mercury Group had taken over the majority share of Phillips, while de Pury remained at the company, as the chief executive and auctioneer.

Arnault's dream of seeing Phillips permanently on the same level as the two larger houses has proved elusive, at least to date. It has been established that an auction house that only works in the upper echelons of the market has difficulty weathering economic changes. It was this, in the end, that led to the failure of both the Geneva-based auction house Habsburg Feldmann and the newly founded ALICE in Paris. The top market sector is difficult by definition, as the two leaders, Christie's and Sotheby's, are particularly strong and the supply of goods is particularly small, and to make matters worse, a company that concentrates on this sector alone can be far more affected by a general weakness in the market.

Content-Related Intermediaries

Museums

Museums regard themselves as research institutions, if nothing else. Their job is to preserve, research, expand, and present collections. Thanks to their scholarship and their authority to define aesthetics—a function that they took over from religious authorities as society became more secular—museums have some indirect influence on the art market, which transcends far beyond their role as buyers. Exhibiting a work of art in a museum affects its market value; selling a piece to a museum elevates the prestige of the work and the artist alike, while the sale is also evidence of the seller's competence (see p. 81 *Museum Documentation*). Furthermore, it turns out that refreshing regional museum landscapes can revive and energize the local art market. London is an instance of this, if we recall Tate Modern, the Saatchi Gallery (originally across from the Tate), and the Frieze Art Fair. Another example is Zurich's Löwenbräu-Areal, which is home to the Kunsthalle Zürich, the migros museum of contemporary art, the Daros Latin America Collection, and leading international galleries.

Owing to the acceleration of technological progress and the increasing average age of the population, museums are actually taking on more significance, since they offer a place to pause for a moment and remember: the antithesis of acceleration and consciousness of approaching death. Moreover, museums as a rule consider themselves an alternative to the commercial art world, and on all levels of activity they insist on differentiating between themselves and the expanding number of market-oriented events. The museum takes objects off the market, effectively wiping out their commercial value. This is the foundation for a hermetic, non-commercial sphere that does not allow for any interaction with the other side.

All the same, museums avail themselves of the art market, and not just when they wish to acquire a work of art. If a museum plans an exhibition and would like to include a privately owned work that is known only because it has appeared on the art market, then dealers and auction houses alike are asked to forward requests for loans to their respective clients. From time to time, even galleries will sponsor exhibitions of artists they represent—these are the ways that the market closes the occasional gaps left by the diminishing ability of government to provide public funds.

Media Coverage

In the more stable art market of earlier times, it was easier to discern changes in direction, and prices were slower to rise. Articles in art magazines or the press in general were regarded as serious instances of "guarding" quality by highlighting the "good" works and artists. Public and media interest in art—and in the art market especially—grew considerably in the nineteen-eighties and nineties. On the one hand, today's market is more short-lived; on the other hand, it is obvious that evaluations of artists and the market value of their art are now essentially a product of the many voices in the media expressing subjective commentary. The influence of this media coverage is strong, but difficult to grasp.

Young artists are evaluated according to the presence of their work in institutions, among other things. This has its consequences, even for the field of art criticism. There is far more regular criticism of an artist's work if an exhibition takes place in a gallery or an exhibition venue, rather than in a museum, because the path from gallery to exhibition venue to museum has also been a traditional test for art in general, with criticism playing an important role. If a new discovery is made by a museum curator and displayed in a museum, where the critique might be less harsh, then an important stage in the process of separating the wheat from the chaff is missing. This can result in art criticism losing some of its significance, if nothing else, with regard to its ability to influence the market.

The Collector as Client

Today's concept of the "art lover" can be traced back to Mannerism. Marked by an enthusiasm for antiquity combined with a high degree of mysticism, this period evolved the notion that art held hidden truths, and that intimate familiarity with it would have a civilizing effect.

The definitive characteristic of collectors is their lasting desire to expand their collection, frequently with little regard to economic circumstances. Above all, this desire is a very special impulse, because fulfilling it apparently intensifies it, rather than satiating it. However, unlike music lovers, for example, collectors seek a lasting connection with the object purchased. Collectors buy art as if it were an artifact that could, ideally, accompany them throughout their life, transferring the aesthetics of the artist's world into the collector's private sphere. As a rule, the individual collector is no longer interested in the purpose for which most of these objects were probably once made; he or she does not want to "use" them. Nevertheless, in most cases, even if a collector takes a piece of art off the market, it is usually only temporarily.

Due to the nature of art, it is not enough to simply purchase a piece of art in order to experience its significance and meaning. Generally, that only happens after one has examined and come to know a work and its context. Since there is no end to the way a work of art can be received, the collector is less likely to succumb to the usual cycle of consumption, in which the consumer buys an item, but eventually feels a sense of disappointment about it and needs to purchase something else—a cycle that the consumer of other luxury goods or branded products can easily fall into. While art can seem an end unto itself, it is the collector's attitude toward art—as mirror image of the usual consumer behavior—that lays the basis for a functioning, constantly expanding market, which in turn lays the foundation necessary for any sort of increase in speculative demand.

If a prominent collector is admired by other collectors, then when he or she buys a work of art, the influence of that purchase on the price of the artist's entire oeuvre cannot be underestimated, since it is comparable to the influence exercised by an important museum when it decides to acquire something. The influential private collector once again plays the role of a trendsetter—a role formerly assigned only to curators. In light of all the empty public coffers, therefore, the collector is more significant than ever.

Another aspect behind the passion of collecting is the way that works of art increase in value. In the eyes of the public and the usual type of passionate collector, at least, there seem to be more and more people who buy art primarily because they are expecting to make a profit or, at the very least, gain prestige, while hoping that it will be as economically sound as possible, too. Frequently, this type of buyer feels less attached to the art than does a collector of the old type. On the other hand, he is interested in titles and labels, lists of earlier exhibitions, and in having the works reproduced in catalogues and illustrated books. On the North American market, the collections that mainly focus on famous names, rather than on the quality of the artworks or the way that they complement each other, are known ironically as "Park Avenue" collections.

Finally, for many, collecting offers a way to acquire a certain kind of posthumous fame, either by publicly exhibiting one's treasures, or by making loans and bequests. Many wealthy people did not become known for their huge fortunes, but for their art collections; even if the fortune vanishes, the collector's name remains linked to the work of art. Opting for the limelight, however, entails a certain risk, since the collector's personal taste and understanding of art will be discussed in public, and portions of one's private life may also be exposed to the public as well. Many American collectors are very willing to exhibit their art collections, and during large exhibitions or art fairs, they will open up their homes to interested visitors.

Important collectors follow the tradition of American donors in believing that a collection is, in the end, just a temporary harbor, because important works of art should eventually be placed in museums. Ultimately, there is also a financial reward in donating to museums, mainly because tax breaks are allowed as soon as an object becomes accessible to the public (see p. 61 *Customs, Taxes, and the Preservation of Cultural Treasures* and p. 81 *Museum Documentation*). Tax advantages range from decreases in the inheritance tax to permitting the entire cost of the purchase price to be deducted from income tax. In Canada and the United States, this goes into effect as soon as the collector transfers ownership of the work to a museum, even if the museum belongs to him—it simply has to be an acknowledged non-profit organization.

Corporate Collections

Meanwhile there is a whole series of corporate collections that are well-respected by experts. They may not have the individualistic charm that accompanies the efforts of the private collector, but they represent a significant demand on the market. For the art market, the importance of corporate acquisitions should not be underestimated: it is believed that, in New York, up to thirty percent of all purchases on the art market (and up to fifty percent in the rest of the United States) are made by corporate collections. Since these collections are being shown more frequently, not just inside the company but also in international exhibitions, one can gauge how much influence these collections might have on shaping the taste of the markets. Not for nothing do American cultural critics talk about the "corporate takeover of public expression and taste"—even in the field of art.

Besides the positive publicity, a company collection can convey the company culture and identity, as well as provide motivation for employees. Today, economic competition not only requires companies that deal directly with consumers to develop a public image of their own, but even manufacturers of primary or intermediary products are also coming under the same kind of pressure. An effective corporate collection can be a subtle, quiet, and indirect tool of communication. It presents the company's origins (including regional) and goals and should establish a corporate culture that is clearly separate from that of its competitors. Therefore, it is very important for a company to make use of the fine arts in a way that allows its image to benefit from the criteria offered by the fine arts—competence, prestige, plausibility, and exclusivity.

Still, a strategy that is mainly concerned with adding to and conserving a collection often results in a company working against a common motivation for collecting, meaning that it ignores the investment potential of art; this behavior is not typical for the art market. It remains to be seen how these collections will be dealt with as the works age, and—in cases where certain works turn out to have a "patina"—if they will be increasingly treated as museum pieces. However, the fear that companies could auction off their art collections during economically difficult times in order to make up for losses in other areas has not, as yet, proved well-founded.

The Dealer-Collector

A special type of collector is the dealer who also collects art, or a collector who makes deals on his own behalf. This group has a few advantages over the private collector: working as an art dealer makes it possible for a collector to have an excellent overview of the market, as well as better access to objects. It is also easier to improve the quality of a collection by exchanging one piece for another, since his sales work expands the collector's own marketing opportunities.

A good example of the dealer-collector is surely Heinz Berggruen, who closed his gallery in 1980 and sold a portion of his private collection to Berlin's Staatliche Museen, some via auction. Another dealer-collector is Charles Saatchi, who has been collecting contemporary art since 1985 and selectively reselling some of it since 1989. By organizing large exhibitions, Saatchi has helped build the reputation of numerous artists in his collection, giving him the aura of a "talent scout." For years he seemed to singlehandedly set the tone when it came to discovering younger artists, and he continues to be an important influence on collectors today. In large swaths of the British middle-class, a contemporary piece now hangs above the sofa instead of an Old Master painting, a transformation in taste due at least in part to Saatchi and his talent for presenting contemporary art to the public as "hip."

Evaluating the behavior of a professional collector depends on one's standpoint. Private collectors disapprove of the business-oriented approach that they believe is behind Saatchi's activities, for instance. Dealers, on the other hand, are pleased by the openness employed by a collector such as Saatchi, when it comes to the mechanisms of the market.

Yet another sort of professional collector is the celebrity who collects and then sells portions (or periods or groups of works) of his or her collection at regular intervals and publicizes their famous provenance. The best example of this is Karl Lagerfeld. The German fashion designer, who lives in Paris, sold his first Art Deco collection at the Hotel Drouot in 1975. In 1991 he sold his Memphis collection through Sotheby's, and in 2000, his collection of eighteenth-century French furniture through Christie's. He also auctioned his collection of Modernist designs through Christie's in 2000, and his Art Deco collection in 2003 through Sotheby's, and the proceeds from each auction were used to acquire new pieces; a typical hallmark of this kind of dealer/collector is that he uses the proceeds of a sale to devote himself to a new field of collecting, in an attempt to function as a "tastemaker," too. This happens at a point in time when a fractional amount of the proceeds from a sale is enough to start building a collection in a new field. Normally, a celebrity provenance increases the value of the objects. However, if a collector's acquisition and sale activities are too heavily influenced by a "stop and go" mentality, then it can have a negative effect on the sales price.

Dealer-collectors have to have the ability to overcome their personal desire to keep something and cultivate the will to part with their pieces, ideally in mercantile rotation. Many people who participate in the market, however, believe that the development of the dealer-collector is a sign that the distinctions between private collector and dealer are gradually vanishing.

Conclusion

The art market is not simply a terminal for a commodity; the gallery system provides a platform for the public presentation and discussion of art. Considering dwindling museum budgets, it is more important than ever that the content of art be communicated. Moreover, the gallery is, as it always has been, the institution that shapes the artist's market prices and strategies.

Auction sales are dominated by the two international companies, Christie's and Sotheby's. Incorporating these two companies into international conglomerates has doubtless led to the recognition or definition of brand name value, the integration of modern marketing techniques from the luxury goods industry, and the continuing globalization of the art market. Still, it has not in fact been possible to successfully dovetail with the luxury industry in order to have access to its customers. For the large international corporations, the art market has proved to be a difficult field, where the rules of market consumption function only to a limited extent.

Apart from the structural changes within the two areas of dealership and auction house, it is also obvious that the boundaries between them are regularly blurred by companies that work with both forms of distribution. As a new profession, consulting also clouds these boundaries even more. So-called art consultants do indeed present a certain amount of competition for galleries and art dealers, but at the same time, they also represent potential demand and have a chance to bring to the market clients who might not have found the way there on their own.

Content-related intermediaries—museums, critics, and collectors—have, on the other hand, contributed considerably to the crucial changes that the structure of the market has undergone since the mid-twentieth century. The situation for museums today has obliged them not only to rent out portions of their space for commercial exhibitions and previews, but also, to a large extent, to ask to receive works on loan from private collectors in order to add to their collections.

The collector uses this development in order to present himself and his collection to the public (with consequences for the market value of the artwork and his own tax situation); corporate collections have optimized this principle under the auspices of public relations.

Media coverage reflects an increasing interest in the art market. Very likely it has less influence on the evaluation of works of art and artists than in the past, although its influence on market relevance and price levels is greater than ever.

These developments have made the relationship between non-commercial and commercial protagonists closer than before. The primary beneficiaries are the large auction houses, which are capable, on the one hand, of drawing a great deal of media interest with their intriguing objects and corresponding marketing strategies, and, on the other, of lucratively exploiting the connection between a work of art from a private collection and its loan to a museum, which increases its value.

Foundations and Frameworks

Organizational Foundations

Philosophers have long grappled with the question of what defines "art." The responses have evolved over the centuries, just as art itself has changed, as if each new generation of artists seeks to step outside the definitions invented by the previous generation. For the art market, however, the definition of art is inescapably bound up in considerations of its value and utility. The ramifications of this are examined at greater length on page 52. For now—like the market itself—we shall begin with a distinctly pragmatic viewpoint on the question of what a work of art *is*: a commodity. How, then, does this commodity reach its audience?

Different Types of Sales

Commodities—whether works of art or any other type of goods—are distributed via markets, and the relationship between supply and demand determines prices. If commodities are not available en masse, but only individually, then there is an unequal division of information between the supplier and the buyer, because only the individual buyer knows how much he is willing to pay, whereas suppliers must rely upon their experience and suppositions in order to determine the maximum amount that buyers are prepared to pay. If more than one buyer is interested in a one-of-a-kind commodity, then the commodity is in short supply.

In principle, the supplier has two possible ways of organizing a sale. A monopolist can set a price for an individual commodity and then wait for a buyer who will purchase it at that price. He can also take advantage of competition among buyers, leaving the price of a commodity up to the bidders' competitive bidding. The first alternative is used in trade; the second, by auction houses. A retailer or wholesaler prices an object and offers it for sale. An auction house estimates the price of the object to be auctioned, the so-called lot. The estimated price can be a fixed amount or it can span a certain range. In addition, the seller and auction house agree upon a limit—that is, a reserve price—below which the lot may not be sold. Ultimately, the highest bid submitted at auction becomes the hammer price of the commodity.

English Auction

At auction, prospective buyers bid against each other. After the bidding process is over, the buyer and the final purchase price are ascertained through a system of rules (established through the conditions of sale set by the auction house). This system of rules allows for every form of auction to be tailored to any purpose. For the art auction, the so-called English auction has become the norm. Here, bidders openly offer successively higher bids, until no one is willing to outbid the highest bid. The seller can establish a minimum bidding price, called a reserve. Bidders are permitted to bid more than once.

Written bids are also included under the category of the English auction. Each bidder submits only one bid in writing. However, the bid that is accepted is not necessarily the highest one. The written bid is more like a limited commission for the auctioneer, requesting him to bid on behalf of the absent bidder. In this way, the written bid is successful as soon as no other higher bid is submitted—that is, as long as the written bid covers the reserve price.

Internet auctions are also conducted in the form of English auctions. The bidding situation is made public by publishing the amount of the most recent, highest bid on the Web site.

On the Value and Utility of Art

On the art market, as we have seen, works of art are primarily considered commodities. However, since the work of art is created for distribution and reception and the artist has to live off the proceeds, the work of art and the market form an interconnected whole. It would be a mistake to believe that the art came first, existed purely, and only the market turned it into a commodity. The market is not the intersection where art and commerce meet. Rather, it is the intermediary that builds the bridges between the art system and the economic system, which are mutually reliant upon each other's existence.

This kind of commodity has two values—the aesthetic and the financial. Both are grounded in the artwork itself and closely interdependent. Buyers, moreover, like to get some utility out of the works of art they acquire. Here, too, there are two sides to their interest: an aesthetic one and a financial one.

As a commodity, the work of art is a durable consumer good; at the same time, it has a material value that can attempt to produce a yield from an investment. Since it is not possible to establish an objective value for a work of art, the economic side is helped by subjectively deciding upon the value of an artwork, which is sustained by the willingness of individuals participating in the market to pay the asking price. As a result, the work of art develops two parallel and interrelated systems of value: on the one hand, its aesthetic value, which is the potential inherent in the work itself and can best be summed up by the term "artistic quality"; and on the other, the work's value on the market. Neither value is a consistent one; instead, both are subject to many different influences. At most, the skill with which a work of art is executed remains stable. In contrast, the way that the artistic quality of a work is evaluated can vary tremendously.

For centuries, the execution of a work of art—the skill with which it was produced—was regarded as one aspect of its artistic quality.

Art theorist Erwin Panofsky coined the concept of the artistic idea, which eventually came to be seen as the actual essence of the work and in so doing diminished the importance of craftsmanship. According to Panofsky's *Idea: A Concept in Art Theory* (1924), this sort of artistic quality is not fixed, but is reflected in the judgment of experts. Their criteria, in turn, are subject to changes in society. The reputation of a once-celebrated artist can decline if it is generally agreed that his work no longer provides any answers to the questions posed by an environment that has been transformed. Conversely, this kind of transformation can also permit undervalued artists to be rediscovered and reassessed. Generally speaking, reliable evaluation of a work requires the passage of time. At some point, every work of art is shifted to a sort of ancestral gallery and takes its place in company with the greats of art history.

Trade value is a neutral value. To a certain extent it is based on aesthetic value, but it is also subject to general social influences, which are separate from the issue of artistic quality. Over time, market players, curators, collectors, and critics come to some kind of consensus about the quality of a work.

The market opposes the notion of "trend collecting," since a trend or fashion is the result of industrialized mass production and it calls for a corresponding type of market. Art, by contrast, is the product of an individual work process. Nevertheless, the art market does entertain some fashionable attitudes that have nothing to do with the aesthetics of a work and, in some cases, are only identifiable from a historical perspective. Only with the passage of time is it possible to determine if the market value of a "fashionable artist" will last. At the same time, the reverse is also true: viewing habits and aesthetic ideas are influenced by record prices, so that market value does influence the aesthetic value of a work.

It is possible to ascertain the price of each and every work of art. As a rule, the price of a work is comparable to that of other works by the same artist from the same creative period that have been made using comparable techniques and are of similar scope and content. This is called "surrogate competition." Artistic quality and uniqueness do not determine each other—after all, many artists have created practically identical renderings of the same subject.

Especially when it comes to Modern and contemporary art, the question of originality also arises, because the reception of art, unlike the reception of other purchased goods, is not limited to a certain time period but rather gradually gathers momentum over time. Therefore, price is not just an indication of artistic quality, but also promises the collector that the best is yet to come.

Moreover, the relationship between utility and value also has a lasting influence on demand. As early as 1899, a study by economist Thorstein Veblen showed that the demand for commodities rises when their price goes up. This so-called Veblen effect also applies to the art market—and it fuels both positive and negative developments with regard to demand and prices. Media coverage of strong declines in auctions and prices might signal to some potential buyers that art is less valuable than they thought it was.

Before the sale of a work, its price is set by the seller, who either sets a (dealer) price and/or agrees to the estimate provided by the auction house. The buyer's interests are only indirectly influential, since the seller is guided by the market—meaning, past sales. However, a sale is still heavily determined by the buyer's motivation. A buyer on the art market may seek aesthetic and financial utility alike, in accordance with the twin values of a work of art.

In art, the main interest is in the mythic and mythological content of the individual work, as well as in the interaction between the work and the observer. According to Walter Benjamin, the original utility value of art is realized through ritual. In his essay, "The Work of Art in the Age of Mechanical Reproduction" (1935), he explains that a work of art only has an aesthetic function when it has an aura. Benjamin defines the aura as a cult value, which is required in order to carry out the ritual. In turn, in order for a work to have an aura, it must be unique and authentic. Consequently, writes Benjamin, technical reproduction destroys the uniqueness of an original work, and therefore, its aura, too. Still—even though the reasons that motivate buyers and consumer behavior are triggered by the notion that the utility of art does indeed lie in the ritual as Benjamin defined it—it is believed that similar behavior can also be instigated by a technical reproduction of a work of art—and not only when the technical reproduction is approved by the artist. This view is shared by philosophers and art critics such as Theodor W. Adorno (who sees the pleasure of reception replaced by "presence," "knowledge," and "increase in prestige") or by Pierre Bourdieu, who, like Benjamin, also regards the ritual as a utility value. Finally, Anne-Marie Duguet even sees this utility in new media art, since this kind of art does not turn the observer into a co-author, but rather, simply makes it possible for him or her to play the artist's game according to the artist's rules.

Added to this is the fact that people who acquire art are generally motivated by a number of factors: self-realization, the desire to decorate one's home, to increase one's prestige, or to invest one's capital. The financial utility of art is inseparable from its aesthetic utility. One of the prerequisites for the ritual is public acknowledgement, which is (also) based on financial utility, even if the latter has not yet been realized. Financial utility is not determined simply by the quality of a work of art, but also by the situation on the market, current trends, coalitions, et cetera. Most consumers are not usually motivated purely by the reception of a work alone. At the same time, owning a piece of expensive art is a sign that the owner is very likely capable of understanding art, since, to outsiders, it seems improbable that the buyer would invest large sums of money merely to give the impression of belonging to the cultural elite. Owning a work of art is accepted as proof of real interest and comprehension. Herein lies the main difference to the "classic" status symbols, such as jewelry, antiques, mansions, yachts, et cetera: the owner of these things is envied by those who share the same notions of value, and the distinction is purely economic. Art, on the other hand, is a "double" status symbol, through which the owner not only demonstrates his financial potency, but also the fact that he has intellectual capacities that most people lack, and this distinction goes beyond economic differences.

The Stock Market and Price

Far more important than the actual purchase price here is the expected market value; works of art that are "guaranteed" to increase in value are nowadays referred to as "blue chips," a term borrowed from the language of the stock market. A prognosticated increase in value justifies even an exorbitant market price, since an even higher price will be paid for the work in the future. An American study has shown that the greater the value of a work, the more likely it is to appear on the market again.

Art market prices have a basis similar to that of the stock market. Determining factors are marketability, availability of works, and the insider knowledge of interested parties, but there are also some factors specific to art: the behavior of those involved is marked by stronger emotional states, as well by their estimate of the value and utility of the art in question.

As far as it relates to the stock market, there is always a reason for high prices on the art market: during "bad times," when stock prices are down and inflation high, prices for art are also high, since money flows into material commodities (negative correlation). When times are "good," prices are high, because art is one of the luxury goods generally consumed when, for instance, stock market profits are easily and quickly made—buyers seeking this type of profit are referred to as "bonus boys." When stocks are up, the demand for art goes up, and so does the price. Works of art become objects for speculators. The difference is that in "bad times" only high-quality wares will continue to sell, while during "good times," even commodities of uncertain quality will sell. This is because when stock prices are high, prices on the art market fall, since money is being invested in stocks. If stocks fall, then investors look for alternatives. The clearer their view of the price/value roller coaster and the accompanying risks, the more price-conscious and critical investors are when it comes to choosing a "replacement market." Another factor with great influence on prices is, therefore, the interest rate. When interest rates are high, art is not an especially attractive alternative investment.

Possibly ever since the stock market crash on October 19, 1987, known as "Black Monday," but definitely since the nadir in 1990, everyone involved in the art market is conscious of the hybrid qualities of the markets. In the late nineteen-eighties it was obvious that plunging stock prices provided more fuel for the art market, since art was seen as an alternative investment at the time. Money taken out of the stock market flowed into art investments, so that the crash actually initiated the art boom. Since then, the art market has increasingly reflected economic and political fluctuations on an international scale: the independent national market is now mostly history.

Art Investment

The great increase in the value of artworks since the nineteen-seventies, at the latest, has also resulted in their being seen as speculative investments. Consequently, investors have created a great demand for information about the attributes and situation of the market, as well as about market developments. Those involved in the market have been glad to comply with this desire for more transparency. The first independent index, the Art Sales Index, was established in 1975. Here, twice a year, art market experts evaluate various fixed categories of goods consisting of thirty to forty works of art each. In order to avoid manipulation, the method for putting together these categories is kept secret, and only the actual assessment is publicized. The most complete and concentrated evaluation is probably provided by the Mei/Moses Fine Art Index, which was developed by professors at the Stern School of Business at New York University. It compares auction results with other economic data and compiles the overall yield produced by works of art that have been auctioned more than once since 1875.

The collection assembled by the British Railway Pension Fund is exemplary of early professional art investment. In 1974 the Fund began to invest some of its cash flow in art. Employing Sotheby's as a consultant, a committee bought all kinds of artworks, which were supposed to be sold off again, over time, and in the midst of the boom in the late nineteen-eighties, a large portion of the collection was indeed sold. Word of a few spectacular sales of Impressionist works quickly spread beyond the art world, and underscored the idea that art was a high-quality investment—and consequently affected the boom. A study produced by the Fund, however, showed that even though profits were higher than those attained from government investments, they were still lower than stock market yield.

Art investments can be assessed like other investment funds and systematically assembled portfolios. Compared to securities, though, it is very difficult to foresee developments, since there is no objective, scientific way to gauge either artistic quality or its influence on further developments. This is because the factors that determine these developments mainly become apparent by examining the past, and they cannot be transposed to the future. When a professional administration is involved in the acquisitions, then works on the art market are divided into safe (blue chip) and risky investments, in the same way that traditional stocks are evaluated. In this case, the safest works are those by artists whose entire oeuvre is already essentially fixed in terms of quantity, and especially in terms of quality. If an international collection is professionally administered in the same way a stock portfolio is, then spontaneous purchases are eliminated as those are the greatest danger to successful investing, even in the field of art. With an art fund, there is no need to worry about the irrational effects of an individual collector's personality. Acting like art dealers, consultants purchase what they believe to be undervalued works of art on behalf of the fund, and they later put them back on the market as soon as conditions warrant. One of the side effects of this is the idea of investing in art production, introduced by French gallery owner Emmanuel Perrotin in 2008: in the classic sort of art investment, investors speculate on the increase in value between the primary and secondary markets, but in this case, investors put their money into the production of the work. The increase in value lies between the production expenses and the gallery sales price.

Nevertheless, the suitability of art as an investment is also determined by certain structural conditions that are themselves independent of market cycles. Regardless of how much revenue is promised, there is an inherent danger in calculating yield. If it is based on a mixed index, then the indicator may be correct, but it might not apply to individual cases. That is why investors must always observe and investigate the specific market they are considering investing in—and not only when making purchases in "unfashionable" areas; generally speaking, more than ever, investing in art must be regarded as a long-term investment. Professional investment and fund planning have exposed the fact that record prices can often be misleading, arising from a particular synergy in the auction room that might not be repeatable. It is clear that the fluctuations of the art market necessitate long-term investment in order to anticipate and counteract opposing currents.

An increase in the market price of a piece of art is not, however, the same as a high yield. When buying and selling at auction, a commission is due in each case. Making it even more difficult, the rate of inflation has to be subtracted from the profit, and one must also take into consideration that one will have to pay to maintain the art once it has been acquired. The negative side of an increase in value, as indicated by rising prices, is the increase in maintenance costs. Expenses for security, climate control, insurance, and inheritance and gift taxes rise in proportion to the value of the work. In order to realize a profit at all, a work of art has to increase in value by fifty percent within five years. Not to mention that art, unlike stocks, does not pay any dividends to its owner. Since dividend-based income has tax advantages for corporations in almost every country, its lack is yet another disadvantage of investing in art, especially for companies.

Legal Frameworks in the European Union and Switzerland

The legal framework for the art market is dictated by national laws. In addition, members of the European Union (EU) must also comply with EU community law, which takes precedence over the laws of individual member states. There are also international protection standards and conventions, such as, for instance, the Convention on International Trade in Endangered Species of Wild Flora and Fauna (CITES), the UNESCO Convention of 1970, and the Convention on Stolen or Illegally Exported Cultural Objects, also known as the UNESCO Unidroit. Demand is also affected by inheritance and tax laws.

Customs, Taxes, and the Preservation of Cultural Treasures

The European Union is a unified customs territory, without internal borders, and it functions like a national market. Each member state levies customs duties, in essence an import tax, on goods imported from countries outside the EU, although the rates (equivalent to that country's VAT) vary; import restrictions for individual countries are forbidden by articles 30 and 34 of the EU treaty.

There are, however, differences in sales, or value-added, taxes. Taxes are due when a sale is made, and actually, compared to other commodities, tax rates on works of art are lower. If the work of art comes from an EU member state, then a reduced tax rate of at least five percent is added to the purchase price. In order for an object to be classified as a work of art and thus subject to the reduced tax rate, it must be the product of an "artistic process." Unlike all of the other EU member states, Germany does not include photography in this category, so photographs are taxed at the regular rate. Similarly, Great Britain has been seen to exclude some installation or minimal art in its classification.

In all of the EU countries, as well as Switzerland, collecting art has tax advantages. As soon as works of art are made accessible to the public, tax law permits the private collector to take a deduction. If a collector should realize a profit after selling an object from his or her private collection, there is no tax on the profit.

Works of art are fundamentally subject to inheritance and sales taxes, and, in Switzerland, even to estate taxes. Owners of artworks must include them (quotas vary from canton to canton) when calculating their estate taxes. Only works of art listed as national cultural treasures are exempted from inheritance taxes in all European countries. If someone has owned a work of art for twenty years, and the art has been accessible to the public for ten of those years, then it is also exempted from inheritance tax, even if it is not listed as a national cultural object; heirs can also make inherited works public after the fact. Likewise, a work of art can be exempted from inheritance taxes if the heirs donate it to the state within a year's time. In France, Italy, Belgium, Spain, Great Britain, and Germany, one can also pay the taxes owed on other parts of an inheritance by donating art objects from the estate to the state.

Exportation of cultural treasures is more or less subject to strict national laws. In addition to national laws, EU directive 93/7 is also implemented. According to this directive, the status of a cultural object is determined by its value. An annex list details all the classifications whose pieces (from a particular value limit onward) fall under the protection of corresponding national laws. Protective measures require that the member state in which the piece is legally kept issue an export license, which is valid for twelve months. If the value of a work of art lies above the limit stated in the annex list—the so-called value threshold—then the owner has to apply for an export license, which involves submitting proof that the object was acquired through legal channels. During this process, national museums can also declare the piece a cultural treasure and thus prevent it being taken out of the country.

In countries where the cultural legacy is one of the nation's most important resources, the laws are particularly strict. State control is very strong in Spain, Greece, and especially Italy. By preventing the transportation of art abroad, the state effectively limits international buying and selling. Also, once one has obtained an export license, one must pay an export tax of up to thirty percent. Furthermore, the Italian government not only has a preemptive option to buy, but it can also confiscate a piece.

Up to now, Germany has allowed the export of artworks based exclusively on the liberal principle of enumeration. Here, works of art regarded by the state as "national cultural treasures" are entered onto a list. It only includes objects in private collections, since the list does not actually provide any sort of substantial legal protection, in terms of historical preservation. The responsibility for this lies with each German state. If an object is successfully registered, then an export license must also be acquired; thus, the registration actually represents a prohibition, but with the possibility of permission. This regulation, however, puts the Federal Republic of Germany partly at odds with EU directive 93/7. This directive was supposed to be integrated into German national law through the passage of the "preservation of cultural treasures" law on August 15, 1998, but since there was no parliamentary majority in favor of it, it was withdrawn.

The value threshold principle has been valid in France since 1992. Here, a new export certificate is valid for five years. Particularly at the highest price levels, the lack of an export certificate can mean a heavy loss in the value of a work; after the state was sentenced to pay reparations in several of these types of cases, the law was revised in 2000. Since then, export licenses for works of art that are more than one hundred years old have been irrevocable and cannot expire, and export licenses for more recent works are valid for twenty years. If the state refuses to issue a license, then it must either purchase the work in question at the international market price or else declare it a cultural treasure.

The United States is the major buyer on the international art market; more than half of all imports worldwide wind up there, and because of this, the United States does not regulate this type of trade at all.

Previously, Switzerland also did not regulate the preservation of cultural treasures. This had less to do with the number of purchases made there than with Switzerland's role as a transit country and shipping terminal for art. In the same manner, the country did not regulate international trade. In 2003, however, the Swiss parliament passed a federal law regulating the transfer of cultural objects abroad, and it went into effect on June 1, 2005. The "cultural objects transfer law" (KGTG), based on EU regulations, implements the UNESCO Convention of 1970 in Switzerland, and its goal is to hinder theft, plundering, and the illegal import and export of cultural treasures. As in the other countries, the law contributes to the preservation of cultural legacies.

The main relevance of the KGTG to the art market is that it controls the export of cultural objects that are on the country's own preservation lists; it regulates claims made on cultural objects illegally exported from Switzerland, as well as the time limit for the acquisition of stolen cultural objects (up to thirty years), and, above all, the law imposes more responsibility on art dealers and auctioneers to exercise due diligence. This made the internationally accepted "due diligence test" standard for every art transaction in Switzerland, too.

Switzerland's most important role on the international art market is probably as an interim depository for art objects. The freeports of Basel, Zurich, Geneva, and Chiasso are tailor-made for storing works of art. Objects warehoused there are not subject to value-added taxes or import duties. Twenty-first-century freeports are service centers for restoration workshops and even galleries, which sell the goods that have been brought there. Sales made within the bounds of a duty-free port have also not been subjected to sales tax, at least up to now.

Droit de Suite

In the perception of market players, droit de suite imposes the strongest limits on market events. Droit de suite is the right of visual artists to receive royalties when their works are resold on the art market. It takes into account the fact that visual artists can only sell their work once, so that, without droit de suite, they cannot profit from later increases in the value of their work. This does not apply to any other type of artist or author, since copyright law enables them to influence adjustments in the value of their works by allowing them the right to grant or rescind permission to use their work, generally by licensing it.

Originally, droit de suite applied to actual pursuit—it was granted to French privateers who were allowed to track down pirates who attacked ships in neutral harbors. The idea to apply this right to works of art originated during the reign of Louis XVI, in 1787. However, it did not actually become law in France until 1920, although it has been in effect ever since.

Many other countries later recognized droit de suite. Germany put it into operation in 1972. Regulations implementing droit de suite existed in all European Union countries, with the exception of Ireland, the Netherlands, Austria, and Great Britain. The latter were obliged to adopt droit de suite through the EU directive of 2001.

Droit de suite is administered in every country by royalty management companies that receive royalties from sellers and forward them to the eligible artists. Successful economic utilization of droit de suite depends on organization, transparency, and, not least, a successful market. In Western industrialized nations, the way that auction houses and galleries are structured makes the art market relatively transparent to tax and finance authorities. That means it is comparatively easy to enforce an artist's rights when it is known that a sale has taken place. As a rule, royalty management companies work with the big associations of art dealers and auctioneers. Royalty rates are usually between three and five percent of the profits from the sale of an artwork. In addition, royalties are subject to sales tax.

Germany's administration of the law has been a model of organization since 1980. Royalty management companies sign contracts with all of the art dealers' associations; these contracts stipulate that the total amount owed by a gallery may be paid annually, at the rate of 1.2 percent of revenues. This not only lowers administrative costs for management companies, but also demonstrates that it is possible to administer the rights of visual artists through an organizational structure that is just as efficient as others, such as the one set up for musicians, for example. Management companies collect royalties, along with contributions to the artists' national health insurance and social security funds.

However, protecting "incorporeal" works such as installations, for example, is difficult. Copyright law does not protect concepts as such. Nevertheless, judgments in various cases have favored the protection of conceptual installations, in cases where the shows have traveled to some extent and the institutions curating the exhibitions have asserted claims to the copyright for the concept. This type of judgment primarily takes into account the fact that more and more installations are turning into stagings, which have been subject to copyright law in opera, theater, and concerts all along. Since the art market does not actually deal in exhibition concepts as such, droit de suite is mainly relevant to descriptions and depictions of concepts, such as drawings and photographs.

Germany's Model as an Example of Art Market Law

With the exception of the business license, domestic trade in art is not subject to any other regulations in any other nation in the world. Auction regulations, however, are numerous, and most are consistent with each other. An example of this kind of domestic legal situation is Germany's method of regulating auctions, which will be discussed in the following.

Germany does not have any special laws regulating domestic trade in art. The concept of the "gallerist" is only legally protected by the constitution, which protects artistic activity (article five, paragraph three, line one). On one hand, the guarantee of artistic freedom regulates the relationship between art and the state, but on the other, it also affects individual rights and applies not only to artists, but also to those who deal in art. There are no other legal regulations, such as laws for protection or control, for instance, so anyone can open a gallery. In contrast, though, auctions are heavily regulated.

At a gallery, a buyer enters into a sales contract with the gallery, which either owns the work or represents the artist if he or she still owns the work. At auction, the auctioneer represents the consignor and requests bids from competing bidders. These bids represent offers to enter into a sales contract. If a higher offer is submitted, the lower one is negated. An auctioneer is not obligated to accept a bid.

The sale of an item must comply with the Sale of Goods law found in the German Civil Code. However, the *Versteigerungsverordnung,* or Auction Act (VerstV), and the *Gewerbeordnung,* or Trade Regulation Act (GewO), determine who may be an auctioneer and under what circumstances, as well as what form a sale may take.

Exceptions are only made when it comes to the way that tax law deals with the art market. In light of the fact that only a small number of artists represented by galleries actually succeed on the market, and that, therefore, galleries must often maintain large, warehoused inventories that cannot be sold at the prices originally anticipated, lawmakers permitted current-value depreciation. This means that the current value of the balance owed can be reduced, which, in turn, usually means that the tax deduction will be far greater than the original cost of the assets. If an object is later sold at a higher price, then the yield is only calculated into the current balance owed.

A license is required in order to hold an auction. This license is issued to individuals and is only granted to natural persons. It will be denied if the GewO has a reason to deny it: the applicant may not be "unreliable" and his own financial affairs must be in order. Such legislation is a clear sign of the government's commitment to protecting buyers' rights and ensuring the legitimacy of the auction as a system of distribution.

Expert auctioneers, in particular, may, upon application, be certified by industry and trade chambers. They must take an oath that they will fulfill their tasks as publicly appointed auctioneers "conscientiously and impartially." "Special" expertise is indicated by professional experience, knowledge of pertinent regulations, and expertise in their particular field. This can be limited, for instance, to art and antiques. Knowledge of the subject must be proved by taking an examination, conducted in front of a committee from the appropriate chamber of commerce. The appointment and oath is of primary relevance to transfers of ownership: if a sale is made by this type of qualified auctioneer, then the transfer of ownership also affects so-called lost or missing items, meaning stolen, looted, or confiscated things that could otherwise not be acquired through sale or exchange.

Consequently, the auctioneer does not mainly appear as the representative of the consignor, but rather, as a neutral authority. In relation to the owner, he is the custodian of the objects that have been entrusted to him. This particular position of trust is protected by law, which is supposed to prevent the exploitation of mutual trust. Lawmakers have also recognized the advantage of selling goods at auction, and have therefore limited this type of sale to secondhand objects. If an auctioneer also operates a dealership, then he is forbidden to auction anything from the dealership's inventory.

The VerstV regulates auction procedures, and its structure follows the order in which these procedures take place. The auctioneer may only take action based on a written auction commission. This commission is a contract between the consignor and the auctioneer, and it must precisely denote not only the type of goods and auction, but also the conditions of the sale. The auction itself can only take place when its conditions have been made public beforehand. Among other things, these conditions determine the division of revenue, the fee structure, and modes of payment. The conditions are part of the sales contract, since they are printed in the catalogue and also displayed at the auction site.

The auction site itself is not regulated. However, the VerstV requires that an estate sale may only contain items that were actually part of the household in question. During an auction, the auctioneer is forbidden to dispense alcoholic beverages in any of the auction rooms.

The auctioneer is only allowed to accept clearly visible or written bids. Accordingly, bids made by telephone are not legally permitted. A bid made by telephone is, by the way, also not "clearly recognizable" as described in paragraph seventeen of the VerstV. This rule can be circumvented if the auctioneer requests in advance a legal, written bid, which can be raised by telephone. The hammer may not fall until the auctioneer has repeated the bid three times without receiving any higher bid. A transcript of every sale must be made. When the hammer falls, all of the auction rules have been complied with. Subsequent activities and business (such as aftersales) are not subject to any special rules.

Legal Framework for Internet Distribution

Art sales have been conducted at a distance, via the Internet, since the nineteen-nineties (see also p. 147 *New Distribution Channels and Trade on the Internet* and p. 166 *The Internet Auction*). However, the application of national laws to business conducted on the Internet has long been a controversial subject among legal scholars and in concrete legal cases. It would seem logical to apply the laws of the nation in which the program is fed into the Net, meaning, the site of the server. From this perspective, however, a seller could simply circumvent unfavorable laws by moving his server to another country. This is why the EU Commission adopted a different model for regulating e-commerce: if the server is not in the same country as the seller, then both the seller and his program are subject to the laws of the country targeted by the content of the program. The content of a program is understood to be tailored to sell an array of goods to the population of a specific country or countries. A primary indication of this is the language used on the Web site. The business operator is also subjected to national law as soon as he fulfills any portion of his services in the country in question. This relates in particular to foreign subsidiaries of American auction houses located in all of the countries where the subsidiaries offer information services, for example, and where they are obligated to pay sales tax on all transactions between the seller and the residents of those countries.

As a result of the argument that Internet auctions must be subject to national laws regardless of the location of their server, the issue of the violation of national regulations governing auctions has arisen. National laws assume that there is a real auction, and that the auctioneer is physically present there. Not only do these laws affect domestic art auction houses, but they have also affected the different national versions of eBay, for instance. However, judicial reviews of the legitimacy of Internet auctions, conducted by a majority of European countries, concluded that these types of auctions are not subject to the auction laws of individual nations, because they are "long-distance transactions."

It is generally acknowledged that a sales contract is agreed upon with the click of the mouse. A contract, however, cannot be validated by a scanned signature; it is only finalized when it becomes a (paper) document, or else through conduct implying intent, such as when the customer pays the purchase price. Still, these Internet-based transactions may be called "auctions." If the seller only makes the portal available to buyers, then he is not responsible for bids made by participants through the portal, as long as he establishes exclusionary rules in his contracts and conducts regular audits of them, in order to prove there has been no negligence on his part.

Illegal Practices

One unorthodox, unmistakable clue that there is resistance to an allocation principle is when it is abused. Auctions, as a distribution method, have received their share of attacks, not least in the form of increasingly sophisticated illegal practices intended to circumvent or undermine the intrinsic fairness of the method; and yet the fact that auctioneering continues is a sign of its robustness, even in the face of competition.

The Mock Auction

The mock auction entails using shills who have no intention of actually purchasing something, in order to force genuinely interested buyers to raise their bids. Frequently, these shills are employed by the auction house, or are relatives of employees.

The classic type of mock auction, however, does not take place on the art market. When a store is being closed, then a "fake" auctioneer and his accomplices pretend to hold an auction. As soon as unsuspecting members of the public come in, the auctioneer sells items at extremely cheap prices to his shills, disguised as bidders. This "bargain atmosphere" creates a sense of excitement that lures unsuspecting passersby into purchasing goods at inflated prices.

Dealers Ring

Participants can agree among themselves to prevent an auction from achieving its goal, namely, to increase the price through the bidding process. If bidders agree not to compete with each other during the auction, in order to have an advantage over sellers and auctioneers, then that is called a ring.

Bidding on behalf of the ring, one member will bid only until the reserve price is reached, while the others refrain from participating. In this way, the ring always purchases items at the level where others, not belonging to the ring, drop out. After the auction is over, members of the ring meet in order to re-auction the lots acquired—only this time, without the participation of the public. This internal auction is called a "knockout." During the knockout, participants take up their positions in order to form a ring, which is where the game gets its name. The original sales price is deducted from the new price, and the rest is divided among the members of the ring. In this way, auction fees and sales taxes are based only on the price paid at the first auction—itself lower than a "market price," since the ring members have agreed to avoid creating competition.

These kinds of proceedings hurt the consignor as well as the auctioneer. The consignor is cheated of that portion of the piece's actual value that was not realized, because of the underbidding. And the auction house does not receive the fees it would have been entitled to, had the bidding been conducted legitimately.

The best protection against these sorts of rings is to establish reserve prices. Since the lot can only be sold at the reserve price set by the seller, at the very least, then the sale is made under the conditions agreed to beforehand by all of the participants. Only a 1927 British law forbids the formation of a ring, and it is punishable by a jail sentence of six months, at the most.

Clearance Sales

An especially popular practice is to sell off an "estate" at a clearance sale/auction. The auction is usually held at an isolated house that is for sale. After renting the house for about three months and putting its original contents into storage, the house is redecorated—that is, it is crammed to the gills with furniture, carpets, paintings, Asian art, and personal items such as jewelry, handbags, luggage, et cetera. These goods are actually items from wholesalers, and many of them are not secondhand at all, but simply patinated, so that they look old. Then the clearance sale is advertised as an estate auction. Goods that are sold are replaced. This system goes on until local demand dries up. In the end, the house is just as full as it was at the start of the sale. Afterward, the inventory is really sold through other auction houses and the house itself is returned.

Other "clearance sales" often involve auctioning things cleared out from the attic of a castle or stately home. In these cases, the things being sold are actually old, but, of course, they are so worthless or damaged that they would have no chance of being sold at a normal auction, even under the "miscellaneous" category. The aura of the castle, however, creates a special atmosphere that makes people want to buy the things from the attic. Especially in summer, these kinds of "stately attic auctions" are very successful, particularly in France and Great Britain.

Conclusion

Ideally, the price of an object sold at auction is achieved through competitive bidding; the English auction is the type employed on the art market, since it has been mathematically proven that this type of auction results in the highest prices.

This does not mean that the allocation principle behind the auction is theoretically superior to other forms of sales. An object can also be sold at auction without any competition. In this case, the price is determined by the reserve established by the seller before the auction—theoretically, the identical process used by a dealer when he sets a price. Whenever a dealer finds a buyer who is willing to pay the price asked, then there is no structural advantage in an auction.

A work of art has an aesthetic and financial value. A buyer is motivated to acquire it for both its aesthetic and financial utility. The behavior of all participants, as well as their assessment of value and utility, is characterized by a high degree of emotion. Value, as well as potential utility are both grounded in the object itself, but are subject to many different types of societal influences, which are, as a rule, generally not recognized until some time has passed. Today, it is acknowledged that artistic and economic worth function symbiotically to create the symbolic value of a work of art.

Added to these societal influences is the economic situation of the art market and other markets as well. On the whole, it is possible to verify that the art market itself—despite its strong decentralization and comparably slow rate of turnover—has been affected by regularly occurring events on the world market, as well as by its economic cycles, ever since the nineteen-seventies. Before then, the art market had mainly been an almost untouched niche market supported by passionate collectors.

As a consequence, investing in art has more than ever become a long-term commitment. Professional investment planners and fund managers have shown that record prices give a misleading impression as to the strength of a particular artist or market sector. It remains to be seen if art only makes a profit in exceptional cases, especially as it costs money to maintain artworks over the entire investment phase. Fluctuations in the art market necessitate long-term commitments, and the buyer must wait out the ebb and flow of opposing currents. It takes considerably more time to carry out an art sale than a stock sale, and an art sale entails obviously higher fees. And, unlike stocks, works of art do not yield any annual dividends.

The market is also affected by different laws in different countries, especially when it comes to various tax systems and export laws. This not only hinders the free flow of commodities, but it also makes it more difficult and expensive to deal in art, or to auction it. On the other hand, the strict regulation of auctions is not a hindrance, but has become a logical accompaniment, and it is of constant assistance in encouraging the "auction mythos." Very generally, Internet art dealers and auction houses have benefitted from globalization. After a valid, harmonized, EU-wide tax system has established and determined the purview of national regulations, these two developments could become models for domestic trade in art.

Art as a Commodity

Product Characteristics

In setting prices for works of art, the same standards are used for almost all kinds of works. Foremost among these is quality: exceptionally high prices can only be attained when something extraordinary is offered. This is not only true for the middle market, but even more so at the top of the market—it can even be worthwhile for a dealer to invest a record price, as long as the available inventory of the artist's work has become so small that any collector or museum wanting to buy will have no alternative but to turn to this dealer. Naturally, intensified focus on major masterpieces makes it increasingly difficult to actually find one.

Generally speaking, it is clear that the buyer is turning more and more to the individual object and away from the ensemble. On one hand, this means that the collector is mixing more periods, techniques, and fields. On the other hand, it escalates demand for outstanding pieces, and there is a growing discrepancy between prices for top-quality objects and those of only middling quality.

Aside from the quality of the work, as well as its size, material, and condition, the artist's reputation plays a pivotal role. Especially to those buyers who want to boast about their new acquisitions, it is important that outsiders see that there is an obvious reason for wanting to own this work. Possession of a so-called trophy picture is a prime way to secure the acknowledgment of society.

Conversely, there have always been certain artists who try to avoid the art market through their selection of materials. To the extent that a work is "ephemeral," it cannot be marketed. Concept Art and Internet Art only occur in the mind and on the Internet, so it is impossible to make a durable commodity out of it, something whose ownership can be transferred. Internet Art is accessible to anyone who has the technical equipment and knows how to use it. In a similar way, this is also true of the increasingly indistinct boundaries between the performing arts, the visual arts, performance art, and last, but not least, the "total installation" (see p. 101 *Installations*).

Authenticity

A work of art must be authentic. Proof of this can be more easily obtained when there is a specialist or a committee of experts that specializes in the work of the artist in question—meaning, that art historians, museums, dealers, and auction houses have agreed that a certain expert or committee is best qualified to judge the artist's works. Reaching this kind of agreement involves a process, and it is also possible for an acknowledged expert to lose his reputation.

If there is no specialist, then, when a work is for sale, it is up to the dealer or the experts in the department of the auction house to establish the authenticity of a work. If there is, however, an external specialist or committee, then all of the works must be presented to it before they can be put on the market. If the expert or committee declines to authenticate a work or provide a certificate for it, then the work can become unsalable, even if the owner and dealer or auction house are convinced of the work's authenticity.

Work by a living artist is a special case. Of course, external specialists in contemporary artists have emerged in the meanwhile, but still, authenticity tends to be determined by the aspects and elements of the works themselves, as well as their provenance. If a work is not signed, however, then, as a rule, caution is recommended: some artists do not sign a painting until it has been fully paid for. Pablo Picasso was especially famous for doing this.

Scarcity

An important factor in determining price is the scarcity of the commodity, because objects that can be easily bought anywhere never have the same allure that a unique piece has. Especially when it comes to auctions, the piece should be unique in order to stimulate energetic bidding; otherwise, interested buyers could simply wait for an identical lot later.

Scarcity is not only based on the existence of a limited number of objects, it also arises when the number of objects has been reduced through natural decay or violence caused by wars and natural catastrophes. In times of need, silver objects were melted down to make coins. Changes in art history have also always taken place at the expense of existing art. For example, antiquities were destroyed during the Middle Ages, Renaissance goldsmiths melted down medieval gold coins, Rococo plaster was destroyed to make way for Neoclassical interiors. Back in the nineteen-thirties, economist Joseph Schumpeter coined the term "creative destruction"—a fitting moniker for such cases.

Market Freshness

The magic phrase for auctions as well as dealers, especially at the big art fairs, has long been "fresh to the market." The longer an object has not been seen in an auction house or at an art fair stand, the greater the buyer's desire. Unfortunately, however, this can have a negative effect on high-quality pieces that have failed to sell at auction and have become known as shelf warmers—nobody is prepared to invest money in pieces that are in constant rotation. Internet databanks in particular can reflect the auction sales prices of pictures for decades, leading to greater transparency over the long run. Every time an object fails to sell at auction, it is documented, and every unsuccessful offering recorded on artnet.com or artprice.com decreases the value of the object.

Famous pieces especially suffer from the fact that they are easily recognizable. For these pieces, the effect of this development is doubled, because the more expensive a picture is, the more likely it is to reappear on the market. Surveys have confirmed this trend, as well as the fact that pictures which have not sold will only realize lower prices.

An owner can balance out this effect if he sends unsold pieces on an auction tour, in the hope that a new target group will know nothing about the most recent embarrassment in the biography of the work, or else has a different sort of taste, or more money than the first group. Hence, pieces that have been unsuccessful in London are gladly sent to the Rhineland, and from there to southern Germany, and then later to Austria and Switzerland—assuming that the streak of failures continues. This practice is less and less effective as the market grows more transparent, and so the radius expands. Buyers in the middle-market segment in Europe are probably not all that well-informed about sales and declining prices in New York, and vice-versa, so that transferring the goods to a different continent can still simulate a whiff of freshness among the regional public, or at least, among private collectors. Another solution is to store the work out of public sight for several years: the assumption is, that after three to five years, market freshness will be restored. Not to forget that whenever the number of buyers increases, then market freshness is naturally less important.

Provenance

Of course, works of art from famous collections have always been especially interesting. In these cases, its provenance enhances a work's other, inherent qualities. It is obvious that, since the nineteen-seventies, celebrity culture has had a massive influence on the auction market especially—beyond the work itself, its provenance is also valuable.

After the crisis in the early nineteen-nineties showed that even outstanding individual pieces had no influence over market trends, international attention was suddenly drawn to historical or prominent collections, and so an interesting provenance gained a great deal of significance in relation to the value of a work. Did a famous person once own the piece? Did the artist choose not to sell it? Additionally, a friendship between an artist and a collector has often resulted in the artist advising or teaching the collector, which can have an effect on the quality of the whole collection—there is a reason for the phrase the "eye of the collector." Moreover, this kind of provenance is the best proof of the piece's authenticity.

Trustworthy evidence of a link to a famous history is therefore important. The work of art itself manifests not only the "idea" of the artist, but also the "idea of famous previous owners"—one is involuntarily reminded of Panofsky's "idea," as well as of Adorno's idea of the ritual. The more famous the history, the higher the price.

Herein lies the reason for the enormous prices that can be realized for the sale of property from important and aristocratic houses. The history of these houses is publicly manifested and is backed up by the public's knowledge of it, which is gained through specialized media coverage. Should society elevate a family of commoners to a kind of aristocratic status, a similar effect follows. One example of this is Sotheby's auction of the estate of Jacqueline Kennedy Onassis in 1996 in New York. The highest price was paid for a necklace of imitation pearls, which Kennedy-Onassis wore almost all of the time and had, therefore, been documented in countless photographs. The necklace, with a material value of about two American dollars, was valued by the auction house's expert at one hundred dollars, but it actually sold for $211,500.

Besides their financial success, these kinds of auctions expand the circle of buyers, and, thanks to the greater media attention, the auction house garners a huge increase in brand recognition. As a rule, an auction of goods from an aristocratic or celebrity provenance appeals to others outside of the usual type of auction buyer, those who are interested in certain aspects of the provenance. These people are frequently novices whose main interest is not in the aesthetic or art historical qualities of the objects, but who are mainly looking for devotional objects. This is due to the fact that, in recent years, interest in famous people and their lifestyles has generally been on the rise, and the media caters exemplarily to this interest; these days, fame is automatically equated with a luxurious lifestyle, which many would be all too glad to share.

Museum Documentation

A sure way to increase worth is to have a documented exhibition of a work, preferably in a state museum, if possible. A curated exhibition in a museum "attests" to an artist's signature, to a certain degree, while positioning the physical object within a body of work—the oeuvre—and canonizing it, making it a part of the cultural legacy. As a result, the renown of the piece expands through the influence of the state, which is generally regarded as neutral. Since the works in a private collection have already bypassed the primary market, it is understood that this way of increasing value can only benefit works by artists who have already achieved a certain amount of access to the market. Also, the greater value of museum documentation demonstrates that more and more collectors judge works of art according to criteria set by museums, setting aside their own, purely subjective preferences. This is also a consequence of the fact that ever-increasing numbers of museum curators are acting as consultants, especially to American collectors.

There can be several reasons why a work has a museum provenance. Either the museum owns the work and may sell it—which is often the case in the United States (see p. 123 *Managing Shortages on the Market*), or the work may have been illegally confiscated from a previous owner and kept in a museum (and, in the best-case scenario, integrated into the permanent exhibition) until the former owner gets it back into his possession and takes it to the market as soon as he can—a typical case of a restitution (see p. 103 *Looted Art as Commodity*). Most frequent, however, are the cases in which a private collection has loaned a work to a state museum. Apart from the factors already named, the work on loan can also benefit from being taken off the market for a while (something not apparent to outsiders), because when it returns to the market, it seems newer. At the same time, the collector has an advantage on the side: his work is stored in a place where it is safe and insured.

There has long been a tradition of exhibiting privately owned works of art in state museums; and ultimately, all public collections were once private collections that eventually became the responsibility of the public. The combination of museum environment (building, quality and type of handling, clientele, and the museum's own inventory, in case there is one) and privately owned works often creates tension between the poles of the familiar and the undiscovered, where the standards of quality are set by the curating done by the museum. When budgets are limited, borrowing works allows the museum curator to close gaps in his or her own institution's collection inexpensively. In addition, the tendency to produce increasingly larger pictures and sculptures also forces collectors to give pieces to museums, since they can no longer fit works into their houses.

Inventive collectors have recognized this as an opportunity to turn necessity into a virtue and still satisfy the demands of a museum, and will take the initiative to lend paintings to museums, or even offer "complete" exhibitions to the curators and management of these institutions. This can easily turn a public museum into a shop window, advertising the collector's goods. In this way, the art market and its preferences can get into museums without almost any filtering at all.

For this reason, museums today are careful when it comes to exhibiting works that mainly come from private collections. Big collectors who want to lend their collections to a museum, therefore, are less successful if they require that the museum take all of the works, or if they want to be able to reclaim their pieces at short notice. As more museums become more reluctant to deal with loans from private collectors, though, collectors are letting go of the idealized image of the state museum and uniting with other collectors to found museums for specific collections, or they are even founding their own private museums.

Classic Fields for Collectors

In order for dealers or auction houses to succeed on the art market, it is necessary to have a sensibility for observing the market, tracking classic fields for collectors, and keeping abreast of trends and fashions.

Painting

As far as the classic areas of collecting are concerned, painting has been the major trend of the past two decades, both on the market and in the art studio. One reason for this is that photography, which was an inexpensive alternative for a long time, is now an established, partly high-priced category; prices for contemporary photographs are almost on the same level as those for paintings. Part of this has to do with the private customer's preference to have works that he can "hang on the walls." It is not for nothing that Anglo-American culture refers to the "wall power" of a piece.

With the appearance of a new type of collector who wants to invest, or at least become well-known, various fashions in collecting developed during the second half of the twentieth century. If a collector is interested in art that does not require a great deal of intellectual effort, then he or she often prefers nineteenth-century art. This stems from a general societal attitude—just as people in the nineteenth century enthusiastically collected Renaissance art, late-twentieth-century collectors were interested in the cheerful, sunny, paradisiacal paintings of the Impressionists. Modern art, by contrast, is just young enough to emit an aura of intellectualism, while at the same time, it is old enough to have been tested on the market.

The first buyers to turn in particular to late-nineteenth- and twentieth-century art were American collectors, who were—and still are—often fascinated by the notion of the artist rebelling against society. The appeal of the Bohemian myth, especially in contrast to the art of the Academy, made them prefer works from the Salon des Refusés to those of snobbish academicism. American buyers also decided to buy Impressionist and Modern art as a sign of rebellion against five hundred years of elitist European art.

Within the field of Impressionist and Modern art, it is clear that, on the whole, the activities of American collectors are supported by their own increasing amount of knowledge. The fact that, as a rule, buyers of Impressionist art are older, more educated, and more experienced is a main reason for the growing selectivity in this area.

For years, the price level for Impressionist works has either risen or been very stable at the least. However, it is obvious that the market is particularly ruthless when it comes to separating first-rate and middling works. American collectors especially have learned (and not just in the first decade of the current century) to be very thrifty and to limit themselves to high-quality works, which are subject to fewer price swings. Signs of fatigue in the mid-price segment of Impressionist art are the result. On the other hand, the attention paid to "tried and true" art after the crisis of 2008–09 has elevated prices for first-rate works to a new level.

New records have also been set for twentieth-century periods and movements: Cubism, Fauvism, Dadaism, Surrealism, Futurism, Symbolism, and German Expressionism. Since the turn of this century, the market for twentieth-century art has been rediscovered, due to the fact that the present-day zeitgeist has rejected the superficial and turned once again to serious work. It is likely that works dating from the second half of the twentieth century alone will, in the foreseeable future, realize higher prices than Impressionist pieces; the demand for postwar art is mainly supported by American collectors, who are willing to pay high prices for Abstract Expressionist works or Pop Art.

Contemporary art has been offered at auction since the mid-nineteen-seventies. The first evening auctions in this field were held in 1994. This was not only a sign of growing public acceptance and market viability, it also proved that dealing in old art alone was not the sole path to financial success.

Logically speaking, though, contemporary art is different from art of other periods in one essential aspect: contemporary art is still being produced, whereas the total number of older works is limited. Therefore, the problem is not so much a question of supplying works in a limited market, but rather the question of selecting works of art and delineating the "quality of art" in general.

Nevertheless, many postwar artists have become so established that a private buyer can feel safe, even without the advice of an expert gallery. Most importantly, though, contemporary works of art have, over the past decade, finally become an established part of the market, with the secondary market partly overtaking the primary. Never before have so many works of this kind come straight from the artist's studio to the auction room, and this has become a strong barometer for emerging art. One of the first highlights of this development was the September 2008 auction of over two hundred works by Damien

Hirst at Sotheby's in London. All of the works were produced expressly for the auction and delivered straight from the artist's studio.

Even though one could defend the position that artists exercise great influence on all of these mechanisms, one frequent criticism is that this turn of events hinders the development of artists themselves, since their style of work has to remain the same, paralyzed in the state that has proved financially successful; an accelerated rate of consumption seems to correlate with increasingly briefer periods of success on the market. This situation has occurred because contemporary artworks have become trappings of social and economic success. In earlier times, it was typically a collection of heirlooms that attested to one's ability to thrive and remain materially successful even under changing social conditions. Since the nineteen-eighties, people who surround themselves with contemporary art receive the most acknowledgment, because not only do they demonstrate that they can afford these works, but they also show that they are capable of recognizing rapidly changing fashions and trends. As a consequence, artists are taking on "star qualities" and benefit from all of the subsequent media coverage or special treatment. More than anything else, an involvement with contemporary art gives the collector the feeling of being a member of a community of initiates.

Media focus on the twentieth-century art market can easily cause one to lose sight of the renaissance of Old Master paintings, which obviously has been instigated and sustained by American collectors. Here, the alliance between private collectors and museum curators has had an especially strong effect. To a much greater extent than the Impressionist trend, the current move leans distinctly toward museum-quality works. To London's disadvantage, this change has also strengthened New York's position as a sales point for Old Masters, even though, as always, about sixty-five percent of the Old Master works on offer come from Europe.

Although the market for Old Masters was considered quite international by the end of the twentieth century, globalization did not really enter the scene until after the turn of the century. Russian buyers, meaning collectors from the former USSR, are as active here as they are in the fields of nineteenth- and twentieth-century art, and their purchases mirror those made in former times, when Russians participated in the grand tradition of collecting Old Masters.

Some might be astounded at the growing demand for old art, since these kinds of pictures often feature unpopular, didactic themes in dark colors. As ever, though, the most important areas of the Old Master market are still seventeenth-century Netherlandish landscapes of the so-called Golden Age, and Italian vistas, since most collectors prefer to live with a Venetian veduta than with Saint Sebastian. These paintings depict the visible world—most importantly, from the sunny side. Just as many Impressionist works do, this kind of art satisfies the longing for harmony and beauty. As far as religious themes go, the only private demand is at the absolutely top levels.

A world-record price paid at a Sotheby's auction in 2002 for Peter Paul Rubens's *Massacre of the Innocents* put an Old Master painting in second place on the list of the most expensive paintings that year. This auction, which garnered a great deal of media coverage, pleased the dealers in this field, who are fond of complaining about the discrepancy between prices for contemporary art and the Old Masters.

There are also trends in content, and when it comes to dealing with paintings, the market has a few bits of lore. For instance, still lifes with dead fish are supposed to be difficult to sell, as are seascapes with storms—collectors supposedly prefer calm waters. The French do not appreciate snowy landscapes, but paintings with dogs "walk out of the galleries." It is said that South Americans will only buy pictures that fit into a suitcase, and Americans are pleased when the Stars and Stripes are part of the painting, especially since September

11, 2001. Blue is particularly popular; subjects in color tests always describe it as "spacious, manly, cool," and so it is especially suited to creating a sense of distance or making a space seem emptier.

Works on Paper

Works on paper comprise an important field for collectors. It is the spontaneity of their creation that makes drawings special; they document the process by which an artist develops an idea, in contrast to the "finished" quality that characterizes the oil painting. Unlike the painting, the drawing is not intended to survive for centuries.

The market for prints seems to have sprung from the success of the prints seen at the documenta 2 in 1959. A special exhibit of *Prints after 1945* was on display there, convincing many visitors that, with just a little effort, almost anyone could become a collector. Works on paper still fulfill this "door-opening" function. The beginner is introduced to modern art and can easily collect and actively participate in the art market. For several years now, photography has been jockeying with prints to be the entry-level item for novice collectors.

A few art fairs, such as London's Print Fair, contest the image of the print as the "country cousin" standing in the shadow of the unique work of art. These fairs address the demands of a highly specialized, knowledgeable clientele. As a rule, this set of buyers is very different from collectors who buy art to decorate their homes—prints and other works on paper cannot be exposed to daylight indefinitely. The print collector acquires works for the collection "in his head."

Sculpture

The three-dimensional experience of space provided by sculpture is very different from the two-dimensional experience of painting, and it can be fascinating for collectors. However, the market for sculpture is rather ambiguous. Only museums have enough room for larger works in particular, but institutions have less and less money for them. On the other hand, smaller works frequently attain record prices, especially when they have a strong effect—"room power," analogous to the "wall power" of paintings. Obviously, three-dimensional pieces are better than two-dimensional paintings at satisfying the collector who enjoys combining different works of art from different epochs. Since 2004 dealers have been reacting to increasing demand by organizing special market forums: for instance, ten of Europe's leading dealers in sculpture now participate in Sculpture Week, which is similar to Print Week or Old Master Drawing Week in London.

Generally speaking, interest in nineteenth- and twentieth-century sculpture is growing in proportion to the ebbing of enthusiasm for older pieces. This is a consequence of increasing unwillingness to confront the religious themes and motifs that comprise the main subject matter of Medieval and Baroque sculptures. As a result, contemporary sculptures are often more expensive than Medieval pieces.

Although they have caught up somewhat, prices for sculptures are still lower than those paid for paintings. The reasons for this might be a lack of space and the fact that paintings seem to fulfill an abstract notion of art.

Design

More and more frequently, the response to the question concerning the hierarchy of form and function is that things no longer simply perform a service. Today, even in low price segments, "design" and "brand" are often more important than the actual utility of an object. Freed of utilitarianism, design objects are now more often regarded as independent works of visual art, and as "design art," they are a combination of sculpture, applied art, purely functional objects, architecture, and construction models. An important role in this process is played by the Design Miami fair; since 2005 it has occurred parallel to Art Basel Miami Beach, and since 2006 Design Miami/Basel has run parallel to Art Basel. It is not just that design dealers are angling for the same customers as the "art" dealers. In order for design to be accepted, it was crucial for these fairs to present design objects in the context of art. Another important factor in the design boom is the general level of prices, which, on all levels of quality, is far distant from the prices paid for fine art.

The highest prices are paid for design art—meaning, for pieces that are acknowledged works of fine art. This is always the case when an artist such as Tobias Rehberger, Mathieu Mercier, or Jorge Pardo designs an object. But how does a contemporary designer come to be known as an artist? Apart from the quality of the art and the originality of the design, there are a few other points. An object may have a recognizable utility value, but that should not be of primary importance—this is a crucial difference from the designs of earlier eras, which, as a rule, were created for industrial mass production. Some of the most beautiful pieces by Charlotte Perriand or even Jean Prouvé, two of the most important designers of the twentieth century, were originally designed to furnish the interiors of student dormitories! Also, the choice of precious materials paradoxically increases the chances that a piece will be classified as art—something like a reverse development in the fine arts, where, ever since Arte Povera at the latest, the value of art has been separate from the traditional, and therefore valuable, product. Today, demand is focused on metal furniture. Diego Giacometti, Alberto's brother, could arguably be regarded as standing at the origin of this development. His Surrealist bronze furniture pieces are strong contrasts to the trends of the nineteen-eighties and nineties—steel tube furniture designed for mass production by Le Corbusier, Marcel Breuer, or Mies van der Rohe. The more hands-on the production, the more unique a piece is, even if it is manufactured as a series. This is also one reason for the success of

Ron Arad, the first designer to reclaim the name of art for his pieces. His aluminum or bronze chairs are characterized by a powerful, masculine, formal vocabulary, while at the same time, their polished surfaces clearly show signs of hands-on craftsmanship. However, the record holder on the art market is Australian designer Marc Newson. His furniture has an aluminum surface similar to the shell of an airplane that has been riveted together, and his pieces are sold at auctions as fine art—the best sign that collectors have accepted them as independent works of art. This demonstrates that, on the design market, contemporary works have also caught up to twentieth-century objects.

Applied and Asian Art

A similar development can be seen in the applied arts. Here, objects are usually bought to decorate one's environment, so that aspects of interior design fashion are emphasized. Hence, this area is particularly influenced by media coverage. In recent decades, demand for traditional wood or veneer furniture in particular has suffered greatly from the fact that lifestyle and décor magazines completely ignore these kinds of objects, or stigmatize them by calling them old-fashioned and boring.

Up until a few years ago, only eighteenth-century goods were acceptable. Nineteenth-century objects were frowned upon, due to the pluralism of styles, early industrial manufacturing, and the simultaneous heroizing of craftsmanship. Ever since the nineteen-nineties "painting prices" have been paid for exceptional, select, and noteworthy French eighteenth-century pieces—meaning, furniture with a historical provenance, made on commission. Since present-day tastes are distanced from the earlier period, and these pieces can easily be integrated, even into modern surroundings, this market sector has remained relatively stable. Weak demand for applied art, as occurred in the 2008–09 season, tends to manifest as selectivity, rather than in lower prices.

Historical products tend to sell because of the fame of their designers and workshops or their previous owners. There is special demand for pieces that do not copy a specific object or earlier time periods, but rather blend the stylistic elements of these epochs into a new kind of furniture. It is reasonable to assume, therefore, that the increasing number of record prices paid for individual luxury items will strongly affect all levels of quality in this sector of the market.

Younger buyers, however, feel that eighteenth-century products are old-fashioned, although they also have not overcome the uncertainty about the nineteenth century. As a result, the market for early twentieth-century applied art is booming. Although this development was visible in the mid-nineteen-nineties, it has clearly strengthened since the turn of the century. Many exhibitions and publications dealing with the transition from the nineteenth to the twentieth century and about the 1900 World Exposition in Paris have contributed to this.

Modern furniture is, in a certain way, the *ébéniste* furniture of the new century and is treated as such, especially by dealers. Mixtures of eighteenth- and twentieth-century furniture are more and more often found at leading dealers, especially Parisian dealers. Prices for first-rate Art Deco objects have been on the level of eighteenth-century furniture since the nineteen-nineties.

On the other hand, leisure-time and "wellness" activities are also influencing the behavior of younger buyers. A desire for antique decorative objects and the dislike for staged rooms full of objects from particular eras often lead them to decorate in country house style, which preferably includes English antiques. One advantage of these simpler pieces is that many are less expensive than modern, manufactured, functional furniture, even when the modern pieces imitate styles of earlier historical periods.

The trade advantage is that the market in this sector is not as transparent as the market for paintings. With the exception of first-rate, signed pieces, it is much harder to trace the path of a piece of furniture or porcelain. Consequently, this market sector still functions in a traditional way; the collector can rarely keep pace with the dealer's background knowledge of the market's history—it is possible to succeed here merely by shifting objects to different regions.

One of the oldest fields on the art market is Asiatica, and it has been experiencing a revival since the turn of this century. The main reason for the enormous increase in prices in recent years is that there is more wealth in general in Asia, especially in China, where, in the meantime, companies and collectors have been purchasing Chinese antiquities with a great deal of knowledge and for a lot of money. Knowledge and financial power are also reasons why the boundaries between valuable, first-rate wares and undistinguished, unsellable objects are very strongly delineated. This is obvious at special events, such as Asia Week in London or New York.

However, when it comes to pieces from China in particular, the "dark side" of the international art trade can manifest itself: many objects were brought to Europe in the nineteenth century by British or French civil servants or soldiers, so that every time there is a big auction, the question of legal ownership arises. Ever since opening up to the West, the country's escalating national self-confidence has been accompanied by an increasingly vigorous desire to deal with these issues in public. An indirect consequence of this new self-confidence is that not only are more private collectors becoming involved, but that also the Chinese government or large Chinese companies are making acquisitions.

Expanding Existing Market Sectors

Existing market sectors can be expanded by enlarging niches. Besides directly expanding business, theme sales also play an important part in aspects of marketing. In their desire to have a share of regional markets, where mid-priced commodities are traded, the international houses have to make sure that they are very well known in these national markets. Once a brand name has been introduced to these markets, then it is easier to start dealing in other kinds of market sectors.

With the goal of establishing twentieth-century German and Austrian art on the international market, and thereby being able to sell it at higher prices over the long term, Christie's started its German and Austrian Sale in 1993. Sotheby's followed in 1997 with a comparable event. As a consequence, the German auction houses, such as the Villa Grisebach, Lempertz, or Ketterer, saw the national market dry up in the top market segment, with justified anxiety. Shifting a limited market sector abroad was dangerous for these houses, since it was not possible to predict if their buyers on the national market would follow the commodities to the international market.

Still, German Expressionist art and artists were not entirely unknown around the world. Even during the period when this art was being produced, international attention was drawn to it through the Nazis' "Degenerate Art" campaign. At the same time, the persecution and flight of intellectual Jews during the nineteen-thirties and forties meant that a number of important artists and collectors emigrated abroad. Above all, auctions and important exhibitions of this art in the nineteen-nineties raised awareness of it, and as it overcame its regional aspects, it became an international phenomenon. This led to new, record prices, not least because droit de suite did not become law in London for a long time. Moreover, the auction format served art historians well, since many previously unknown works were made public through their documentation in an auction catalogue.

On the other hand, transplanting a national market to someplace like London is always fraught with risk, since the change of locale brings with it other determining factors (not completely unknown to the previous participants in the market), such as foreign economic cycles and fashions in collecting. There is, however, a plus side for the trade: national markets are inexpensive places for international dealers to make purchases. The positive results of the German Sales led to other national auctions, such as Italian Sales, Irish Sales, Greek Sales, and Scottish Sales.

The London auction firms, however, soon realized that, especially in the middle market, they could not attain higher prices than their German counterparts, which made it difficult to argue in favor of a London sale with a consignor. On the other hand, since the London auctions were supported by sales of top-level paintings, it was particularly easy to see the market drying up, not to mention the buyers' growing reluctance to buy. After ten years and countless record prices, therefore, Christie's and Sotheby's changed their concept. Using the argument that German art had achieved international recognition, in 2003 they stopped the German Sales in the mid-season format, and made the category a part of the regular Impressionist and Modernist auctions.

New Areas of Business

One characteristic of the art market is that there is always a shortage of goods. This has two consequences: for one, it justifies the high prices that are paid when a masterpiece actually appears on the market. For another, commercial art dealers look for new customers by opening up new distribution paths, such as the Internet, and christening more and more commodities "art." The first step entails the provenance-driven "showbiz" auctions held by the international auction houses. In the meantime, anything that even gives the appearance of having an art connection goes on the auction block. Just a few years ago who would have thought that art auctions would feature leftover pieces of Russian space capsules, replacement parts for the Concorde, or James Bond movie posters?

Ideas for these types of collections come from all areas of pop culture and are therefore not only more numerous, but also easier to plan and market: to do this, the "memorabilia" trade uses the same tools available to the sales and marketing departments of, for example, record companies. Ultimately, these areas, which one would think would be highly dependent upon trends, are, in reality, very stable. Extraordinarily high, headline-making prices are the exception; price levels normalize after a short while.

Shrinking Markets and New Trends

Of course, a market sector does not naturally cease to be when all of the masterpieces have disappeared from the market. If the market shrinks due to a lack of available goods (which can cause values for dealers and owners alike to rise), then beginners are warned and look for other, less constricted fields.

A shrinking market puts dealers in an advantageous position in relation to the segment of the market that is affected. Since no auction house can hold an auction with three masterpieces and a lot of filler, and it is too dangerous to integrate one masterpiece into a group of ordinary works, then a dealer's special knowledge and his ability to market a single masterpiece by itself is a great advantage. Thus, it makes sense that a shortage is especially noticeable in the auction catalogues, while dealers can decorate their showrooms with warehouse inventory for a certain amount of transition time. As a rule, if an area disappears from the assortment at the big art fairs, the end of a wider supply is imminent.

As one sector closes down, collectors often shift their interests to a related field that has received less attention. Hence, when paintings are expensive and in short supply, a collector of Old Masters may concentrate on Old Master prints and drawings. Prints, especially, used to be looked down upon as mass-produced goods; at best, they might find their way, unchallenged, into museum collections. Since the nineteen-eighties, however, there has been a clear increase in interest and prices.

When the international market takes up a new field, the first consequence is that prices paid in the beginning will be higher than any price that the artist or even a gallery could have demanded for work from this field. Generally, trends are created by the international auction houses, which have ways to contact buyers and the money necessary to do so, and these can be used to communicate an idea to a large, international public. Here, we see yet another side to the problem of acquiring new blood on the art market. The less knowledge collectors have, the easier it is for auction houses to create trends and turn everyday objects into "art." As a result, in these areas, dealers' knowledge of art history counts for very little.

Even for the smaller auction houses, however, this development might be disadvantageous. They cannot create trends on their own, as they do not have the marketing tools and the attention of an international public. And since sellers frequently tend to offer the large international firms objects that can be sold abroad, then they also have an advantage when it comes to acquiring supplies in their newly created fields. Dealers and smaller auction houses are left with the market niches that are not lucrative enough for the big firms, but in which a dealer can definitely establish a monopoly.

Photography

It took a long time for photography to become an acknowledged art form. Up until the nineteen-fifties there was no particular market for the products of this technology, which was over a century old by then—and which has now long been replaced by its digital form. In the meantime the demand made by contemporaries of the inventors—that photography be valued on the same level as painting—has been fulfilled, and for many years now the market has recognized photography as an artistic medium. As far as the art market is concerned, photography is usually a field for beginning collectors, and it now competes very successfully against prints for buyers.

The market has gotten around the problem of originality by defining terms that are supposed to reassure buyers about the number of prints that have been made of a photo. "Vintage prints" are defined as having been made within the first five years after the negative was produced, usually by the artist him- or herself. Normally, there are so few of these that buyers will also accept prints in poor condition. "Period prints" are those that were made for commercial purposes after the initial five years; if more than ten years pass between the time the photograph was taken and the time the print is made, then it is labeled a "modern print." Finally, prints made after the death of the artist are called "estate prints," if they are commissioned by the trustee; otherwise, they are simply billed as "later-printed prints," which can sometimes be distinguished by their narrower spectrum of tones. Just a few photos have an edition number at the bottom edge of the picture, as prints do; this is a sure sign that the prints were made specifically for the fine arts market.

Traditionally, fine arts photographs were sold by dealers. It was not until 1971 that Sotheby's held the first photo auction. In Germany Hauswedell & Nolte have been offering photography as part of their modern art program since 1975, and in 1976 Lempertz held the first photography-only auction. Photography premiered at Art Basel in 1998. As has long been the case, the United States is the major market for photos. One factor in this might be that the medium was first invented only some fifty-odd years after the establishment of the United States itself, and it was thus easy for the young nation to embrace the new technology, which came without the burden of centuries of Old World history. In addition, the conquering and industrialization of the country was documented in photographs, which were not burdened by European art traditions—photography was accepted as a typically American medium.

Early collections tried to represent the history of the medium from its invention onward. Since prices have risen so much, this is almost impossible to do anymore. As a result, people collect the works of certain photographers, their schools, periods (e.g., Surrealist photographs), or motifs. After 2000, when the magic threshold of one million dollars was crossed (paid for a photo by Man Ray), it was just a question of time before the gap between the prices for photography and contemporary art in other media closed; after all, photography has kept up the fastest rate of growth on the art market for a long time.

So, outside of auctions and galleries specializing in photography, photos can mainly be found in galleries and at auctions where contemporary art is also sold—photographs represent up to one-third of the items at contemporary art auctions held by the big firms. For the field of photography, this means that buyers purchasing photos think of themselves as collectors of contemporary art, and not strictly as collectors of photography—something they are not and do not want to be, either. Other typical purchasers of photography at contemporary art auctions are buyers of trends, who do not collect either art or photography, but are simply interested in the medium itself. Neither group of buyers is consistent in their purchasing habits.

Having been acknowledged as an art form in museums and on the market, photography has gained a new, unconventional aura. In addition, the first signs of a slowdown are emerging in this new field; nineteenth- and early twentieth-century photographs are appearing less frequently on the market. Second-class works on the market are not only inferior in terms of artistic quality, but also in terms of their physical condition, which is becoming increasingly important. Gaps continue to be filled by press photos, which proved that they could also realize high prices during the frenzy of the nineteen-nineties. If these pictures are sold by photography agencies or newspaper archives, then occasionally the courts have to decide if the archives are legally allowed to sell them, or only publish and store them. Amateur photographs, either by unknown photographers or even by automats, are also treated in the same way; if they date from the late twentieth century, they are often Polaroid Instamatic pictures. Generally speaking, older photographs tend to be sold in London, while contemporary prints are usually offered in New York.

Finally, in recent years there has been much stronger awareness of the importance of properly storing works of art; the condition of a picture has increasing influence on its price. Ultimately, photographs are made of very diverse types of paper that have been exposed to chemical substances and light. Preserving color photographs on paper containing various plastics is especially difficult. Photographic works of art need to be kept in rooms where the temperature is, ideally, a constant 8 to 10 degrees C (45 to 50 degrees F), otherwise, signs of damage will appear within a few decades. Exceptions are silver gelatin or platinum prints, which are clearly more durable.

Escalating interest in photography has led to the emergence of various institutions that offer commercial wares, as well as places for education, research, and conservation. New York's International Center of Photography combines a museum with an educational and research facility, as does the Swiss Foundation of Photography in Winterthur. France has been particularly active in the domain of photography, with several major festivals, trade fairs, museums, research and conservation centers, and schools devoted exclusively to photography. Among other European institutions, the University of Zurich and the University of Paris VIII offer the possibility of studying the theory and history of photography as part of both their bachelor's and master's degree programs.

Installations

Originally, artists worked with small installations that combined just a few objects and therefore could be moved and sold as if they were sculpture. More difficult to deal with were works that leaned against the wall, took up part of the floor, or even filled an entire room. Still, within a narrow-enough framework, even these types of installations could be dealt with. In these cases, the way that the artist has arranged the works is indispensible, even a part of the work itself. The space surrounding the objects is a neutral shell and can therefore be changed; possible buyers may not only include museums, but also private collectors with sufficient space to house such a work (or at least, the willingness to loan the installation to a museum).

At the foreseeable end of this development, however, is the "total" installation, which includes the space itself, and therefore becomes immobile: the installation is made up of the entire space and its contents. It is difficult to see how these "total" installations could be sold—but some artists do this deliberately, in an attempt to criticize or circumvent the art market.

New Media Art

In contrast, new media art has proven to be marketable, despite all of the critical voices. Video art has long been a major genre in contemporary art; young artists in particular employ this technology as often and as self-confidently as paint and canvas. This is more obvious than ever since the documenta 11 in 2002, which went down in the annals of art history as a triumph of video art. However, it must be said that works of art based on video find it more difficult in general to assert themselves in the face of the advertising industry's aggressive use of video. At the same time, more of these kinds of works require explanation and therefore underscore the role of the gallery.

In the meantime, the work of early media artists is now subject to the same rules of the market usually applied to art in classic media. Experts are still uncertain about how to evaluate avant-garde art, if the artists are using new media, and especially if the works are interactive. This reserve on the part of critics has an effect on the art market. It is one of the major reasons why videos are still marketed by large non-profit organizations, which act like video stores that loan or sell works for a small amount of money.

Also, the percentage of private collectors remains relatively small. Only a few people surround themselves at home with slide projections, videotapes, and video installations, partly because even if there is no film running, the machines necessary for showing it are ordinarily quite visible.

Another hindrance is that the electronic data of a work is not in a form that can actually be signed. Unlike a photo, there is still no way to link a signature to the work of art itself. So far, the art market has not accepted any sort of link between a signature and an electronic image, which means that sometimes the work is denied the value given to an "original."

Another problem arises when a work needs to be restored. Early works in particular often age very badly and need careful, extensive restoration. If they have been stored improperly, video tapes will show signs of damage after just ten years, and only regularly scheduled transfers to an updated system can stop this. Since damage to the picture and sound can influence the appearance and statement of a work, digital retouching must also be carried out on a regular basis; the boundary between this and forgery has not yet been defined by art historians or the market. It also remains unclear who is responsible for the costs of restoring a work—does the purchase price merely cover the lifetime of a magnetic tape?

Looted Art as Commodity

Generally speaking, looted art is any object that has been taken from its legal owner through an act of war. As far as the art market is concerned, the most relevant commodities are cultural objects that were illegally taken or confiscated during and after World War II. This includes works of art that were confiscated because the owners were persecuted as a consequence of the anti-semitic, racial, or political policies enacted by the Nazi authorities during the Third Reich, or works of art branded as "degenerate" by the Nazis, as long as they belonged to private parties. Finally, spoils of war looted from public institutions by members of enemy armies are also classified under this rubric.

If a former owner can identify objects and prove his or her claim, and if the objects are in the possession of a public institution, then a civil court can order that they be restored to the rightful owner. Restitution cases have also concerned former property owners in East Germany and other central European countries where Communists confiscated private property after 1945.

Theft and Restitution

National Socialism extensively affected the cultural world and the art market. Forming a new nation meant "cleansing," regulating, and monitoring cultural life. Artists who were practicing Jews or of Jewish heritage, or "Aryan" artists whose art did not serve the ideological ideals of those in power were branded as "degenerate" and forbidden to work. Undesirable museum directors, curators, and professors were fired. Everyone who worked in the fields of fine arts, music, film, radio, theater, journalism, literature, architecture, and the art trade was forced to become a member of the Reichskulturkammer (Reich Chamber of Culture), founded in 1933. Membership was only open to "Aryan" Germans or those whose art was politically and artistically approved by the regime, while at the same time, membership was required for anyone who wanted to continue working in his or her profession.

Following the institution of these regulations, a wave of experts was forced out of the cultural arena and the art trade. At the same time, "degenerate" artworks were removed from museums and collections and publicly destroyed or sold abroad at fire-sale prices. Due to its neutrality, customs regulations, and lack of trade limitations, Switzerland became the destination for many of these objects. As a further means of vilifying the art they disliked, the National Socialists organized the *Entartete Kunst* (Degenerate Art) exhibition, a propaganda tool specifically curated to ridicule the contemporary art of the time. It went on display in Munich in 1937 and then traveled in a modified form to various cities in the German Reich.

Private collections owned by Jews suffered a similar fate to museum collections; after Jewish citizens were excluded from economic and cultural life immediately following the National Socialists' ascension to power, many people who owned works of art had to sell them to pay the so-called flight tax and to support themselves in exile abroad. Art that falls into this category can be subject to a restitution claim.

Ever since the end of the war, victims have attempted to retrieve objects lost from their collections. Since a large number of works were "legally" confiscated, these demands were rejected in German courts in early postwar years. In cases where a claimant's suit was successful, the object itself was not returned, but compensation was paid instead. Even after the end of the war, doubtful practices continued. In an attempt to keep important (confiscated) works of art in the country, Austria, for example, sometimes only issued exit visas or export licenses in exchange for "donations" of some of the works in question. As a rule, the Allies did not return stolen works of art to individuals, but to countries. Works that could not be returned remained in Germany and were given to state museums, where they were kept as "loans from the Federal Republic of Germany." This was also the case in France and the Netherlands.

Toward the end of the twentieth century, public interest in the complex topic of looted art increased, and the number of restitution claims rose. There are many reasons for this development. Firstly, after many archives were once again opened up to the public, it was at last possible to do in-depth research. Secondly, the archives of the former East Bloc countries, most of which were not accessible before 1990, also opened up, and lastly, German reunification led to state-sponsored investigations of the objects and documents found in institutions and archives. In addition, the Internet now accelerates the spread of relevant information.

In addition, more works of art, once considered lost, came on to the market or were shown in exhibitions after the former Communist countries opened up. A number of new publications investigated art thefts committed under the Third Reich; standard works have proven to be Lynn H. Nicholas's 1994 book, *The Rape of Europa,* and Hector

Feliciano's report on confiscations in France, *The Lost Museum,* published in English in 1997. Consequently, not only did public interest increase, but there was more pressure on institutions to deal with their role in the Third Reich and their later handling of looted objects. Last, but not least, the fiftieth anniversary of the Allies' liberation of Germany made it clear to many that it was finally time to redress the injustices of the war.

In December 1998 the Washington Conference on Holocaust-Era Assets was held, where it was decided to establish a framework for "disclosure and restitution," and these fundamental guidelines were reaffirmed in the Terezin Declaration issued by the follow-up conference in Prague in 2009. The countries affected deal very differently with this burdensome legacy. Generally, ever since the French national museum was opened at the Louvre in 1793, one of the tasks of museum curators has been to research their collections, and this includes provenance research, i.e. recording the history of ownership changes and the origins of works in the collection. Yet, right after the war, none of the museums in the Federal Republic of Germany, other European countries, or in America undertook investigations of their collections in order to identify looted works of art.

In Austria in 1996 a separate group of artworks, which had been identified as looted art but whose owners were no longer to be found, were auctioned by Christie's for the benefit of the Jewish Community in Vienna. It was the first auction of returned objects to be held in the postwar period. Sensitized by this auction, and put under pressure by parliament, the Austrian federal government decided in February 1999 to return to the original owners or heirs all of the pieces that had been extorted from them in the postwar years and were now in federal museums. In addition, a federal law was passed in 1998 that gave museums the funding needed to research the provenance of works. This process was considered a model for other European countries.

In the Netherlands, the Rijksmuseum in Amsterdam led the move to investigate the state art collections; an ethics commission was established which had the authority to restore works of art to heirs. A final report, published in 2000, showed that ten museums had works that had been confiscated during World War II by the authorities of the German occupation and then turned over to the museums. In Great Britain, the National Gallery began its research in March 1999, and the Tate Gallery, the Victoria & Albert Museum, and other institutions followed suit that same year. In France, the Musées Nationaux Récupération (an inventory of works looted in World War II) was also investigated by an ethics committee. In 1996, after countless headlines about "Nazi gold" in Swiss bank accounts, Switzerland instituted an independent commission of experts (dubbed the UEK) for World War II, which also shed light on Switzerland's role as a collection point for looted art. Since the 1998 conference in Washington, almost every museum in the United States is engaged in its own provenance research.

In Germany, following a joint declaration made by the federal and state governments, the museums in Berlin, Cologne, Dresden, Hamburg, Leipzig, Munich, and Stuttgart took on the duty (identified in the declaration) of investigating their inventories for pieces that may have been confiscated by the Nazis. In addition, the Lostart Internet Database (www.lostart.de) was created under the auspices of the Koordinierungsstelle für Kulturgutverluste (Central Office for the Documentation of Lost Art), and museums were granted state funding for provenance research. Many individual projects for provenance research were also carried out; the goal was to find the owners of the artwork, rather than oblige the owners to search for their works themselves. Knowing that exchange and networking is especially important to provenance research, events and conferences have been established in order to accelerate the exchange of information, such as, for instance, the Arbeitskreis Provenienzforschung (Provenance Research Working Group), founded in 2000.

Sources for this research are the works of art themselves, with their labels, stamps, or signs, as well as inventories of collections, documentation of objects, correspondence, photographs, and public archives. Others are artist monographs, catalogues raisonnés, exhibition and auction catalogues, magazines and newspapers, Internet databases, and historical witness accounts.

Legal Bases

At the forefront of these conflicts over looted works of art is the question of what constitutes legal ownership. As far as the investigations are concerned, the destruction and loss caused by war and the problem of deceased witnesses mean that investigators have to accept that, on occasion, it is difficult to pursue justice under circumstances where the facts are only rudimentarily clear. It is easier to file a claim for restitution when a collection has been well-documented. However, even though the amount of time that has passed has opened up previously closed archives, the statute of limitations has run out in many cases.

As a rule, the restitution process is an international one. Either the works of art or the owners, or, in most cases, both, have survived an international odyssey. When it comes to international civil law, jurisdiction is always held by the country in which the object itself is located *(lex rei sitae)*. However, if the event to be investigated has taken place in another country, then that country has jurisdiction. Beyond the investigation of these circumstances, the transfer of the object to another country brings with it a so-called change of statute, so that further legal action can only be taken according to the laws of the country of *situs*. When it comes to assigning jurisdiction, the legal concept of *ordre public* allows some European courts more room to play; *ordre public* entails the idea that a foreign judgment has been obtained fraudulently, while violating "public policy" at the same time.

It is possible to see the gaps among all of the national legal systems when an individual country permits the good-faith purchase of looted objects; this means that, under certain circumstances, a buyer can legally become the owner of a looted item without having to face any objections. In this situation, however, the buyer has certain obligations to exercise due diligence; when acquiring works of art, the buyer must, for instance, inquire into the origins of the object and verify its provenance through sales contracts, customs or insurance documents, or invoices from moving companies.

The more professional the buyer, the more important it is that these requirements be met. Dealers and museums are obliged to pursue in-depth research if there is any specific reason to be suspicious about the object's background. Even for private parties, however, the pressure to exercise due diligence is building. A buyer (or provenance researcher) can be assisted in the research task by Internet databases, such as Interpol's Art Loss Register (ALR) or www.lostart.de; such databases gather and publish information about works of art that have been reported stolen. Also, to support this kind of research, many museums publish their inventory lists, along with provenances; the American Association of Museums, for instance, operates a database under www.nepip.org.

If an object has been taken from an owner either by theft or fraud, for example, then in many jurisdictions it is usually impossible to make a purchase in good faith later. Since the Nazis were allowed to appropriate works of art under the laws of the Third Reich, and these laws were either unjust and therefore invalid even at the time they were passed, or else declared void under substantive law by today's courts, then it may be considered clear from the outset that they were not to be respected.

Under certain conditions, however, the legal systems of several countries also recognize that there are exceptional cases in which a lost or stolen piece of art has been purchased in good faith. Italy, Switzerland, and Germany permit this, for example, if an item is purchased at a public auction or if it has been in the buyer's possession for a certain amount of time, as established by law—the legal term for a change in ownership of this kind is "adverse possession." If a buyer has purchased something legally and in good faith, then he is permitted to legally transfer it, even to countries whose legal systems do not recognize good-faith acquisition of stolen or lost objects.

How This Affects the Art Market

Restitution claims have raised the bar in relation to sales of works of art: every time a piece is offered for sale, there is a risk that a former owner will see it in a publication, often in a fair or auction catalogue, and then file a claim to it. Even if these claims are ultimately unsuccessful, this type of third-party title claim can take an enormous amount of time. Also, anyone possessing a looted object and offering it for sale can be prosecuted for receiving stolen goods.

For these reasons, companies involved in the art market have developed mechanisms for verifying the background of works offered to them, and large auction houses have their own restitution departments. First, publicly accessible databases are scanned to see if the object appears in any of them. Since the 1998 Washington conference, dealers and auction houses have been under far greater obligation to investigate the background of an object, and so simply searching the Internet databases for objects is no longer considered sufficient. If the object does not appear in any of these lists, then gaps in the known provenance are researched further. There are also lists of victims' names, as well as lists of people who are known to have been involved in the confiscation processes during the Third Reich. If it turns out that there is indeed a gap in the provenance or a link to one of the registered names, then an investigation into how the work came to be lost is begun. Although a gap may indicate a theft, it does not prove one. Was it stolen or sold? Was it an emergency sale, because money was needed; was the owner forced to sell? Finally, another search must be conducted in order to find out if a member of the family has already filed a restitution claim, probably in the postwar era, and has already been recompensed for the loss. None of this, however, excludes the possibility of natural restitution, i.e., the restitution of the object itself. If it is established that the object is indeed a looted object, and that there has not been any recompense for the loss, then an investigation must be made to discover if there has been a good-faith purchase in the chain of later transfers of ownership.

If, after all of this research, the restitution claim is still valid and the work is in the hands of a private party, then the dealer or auction house can, at the behest of the owner, negotiate a dialogue with the former owner. The two parties then have an opportunity to agree upon a contract that will regulate the valuation of the piece and the distribution of any proceeds from the sale. Information gained through the provenance research is printed in the auction catalogue, as legal proof.

In this process, the position of the auction houses is that, according to the nature of an auction, the firm does not actually own any of the objects to be sold, but rather acts as an intermediary between the seller and buyer. A dealer, on the other hand, buys works of art and is therefore also the seller, and if, after seeing an object in a publication, the former owner comes forward, the claim is filed against the dealer. Thus, it has been claimed in the media that the public nature of the auction is an appropriate way of resolving cases of art theft perpetrated by the Nazis.

As state-run museums began conducting their own provenance research, freelance researchers also became active in this sphere. These independent researchers investigate the whereabouts of artworks and attempt to have them returned, earning either a percentage of the proceeds in successful cases, or an hourly wage, if they have been hired by attorneys.

All of these examples entail the sale of a work of art that has been returned. Research, negotiating the restitution, and lawsuits usually cost so much that, after an object has been restored to the owner, he or she is forced to sell it out of necessity. Also, the rightful owners are often numerous co-heirs, who may wish to divide the proceeds among themselves.

Obviously, this development can negatively affect the image of market participants. On the one hand, more evidence that the European auction houses cooperated with the Nazis keeps emerging, showing that they were an important element in the market for stolen art. Even famous art dealerships have had to acknowledge that their trade aided or supported the Nazis in their confiscation of art between 1933 and 1945. On the other hand, the "looted art shadow" can fall upon a work before it goes to auction and thus hinder or prevent the auction, if the former owner withholds knowledge of the piece's whereabouts and goes to court in an attempt to stop the sale. Although claiming restitution after an auction can no longer prevent the business from being concluded, it is likely to damage the auction house's image, making their research methods look insufficient and careless. If an owner has a piece with a mysterious past, which may conceal a Nazi crime, the publicity may prevent him from trying to sell it. Therefore, experts believe that looted art with a murky provenance is essentially unmarketable.

Works of art or collections that have been returned to owners are first-rate commodities on the art market. They are often high-quality objects, and this means that they have been collected and documented throughout history (which makes them easier to find and identify). They are also naturally extraordinarily "fresh" goods on the market. A third advantage is their provenance: either a famous collector or even a dynasty has come into possession of objects from famous collections, or else they come from museums.

If this collector cannot be found (or wishes to remain anonymous), the good name of the museum where pieces have been maintained in the collection or storage carries its weight. Other qualities also make returned works of art valuable commodities. Provenance research undertaken as part of the restitution process makes it easier to investigate an item's authenticity, or even prove it entirely. If the objects have been in a museum since World War II, they have, as a rule, been thoroughly researched by experts, while many of them have been restored and are rarely moved, so that they are in especially good condition. In addition, ownership has been legally established. The objects are once again fully marketable, and buyers will acquire the "good title," meaning the indisputable property rights.

How can one proceed against trade in stolen art? Auctions houses and art dealers protect the information via constantly updated databases such as the Art Loss Register. In the future, it would be helpful for dealers and for the auction houses in particular if a single database could gather and publish all the information about Nazi looting that has been collected to date by the various groups researching the subject.

Art Forgers

Forgery shadows art. Just as the subculture of illegal auction practices underscores, in its own peculiar way, the power of the auction as a model of allocation, the forgery of an object is an expression of its expected success in the appropriate market segment. In a period in which the specific notion of "original" is a theme of art itself, and partly under fire to boot, the reverse is also true: the desire for authenticity is more marked than ever. Yet, even for experts, it is not always easy to establish; the critique of style and scientific methods are of assistance to art historians here. At the two opposite ends of the poles are the great skill of the forgers and the great knowledge of the experts. Clever forgers produce the precise "truths" that fit into the narrow perspectives of experts; the forger is an opportunist par excellence. Experts' firm belief in their own infallibility actually allows forgers to victimize them.

Moreover, experts frequently debate the various methods of art historians and scientists. Most controversial are the methods used to determine the age of a piece by measuring radiation (carbon 14 dating and thermoluminesence). Critics contend that ionization can expose objects to so much radiation that measurements can be inaccurate. The age of metals, especially bronze, which has been used in sculpture since classical times, cannot, in general, be scientifically determined—provided that a forger has used an alloy that was common in the period in which the documented original was made. Even if the age of the material can be determined by measuring residual moisture, for instance, that still does not answer the question of when the work was actually carried out.

Marks on the canvas and stretcher, estate stamps, or exhibition labels are relatively easy to identify. In terms of the structure of the picture, though, an expert who is familiar with the technical side of painting is required, someone who knows how a painting is made from the ground to the brushstroke. Looking at the paint through a microscope provides technical information about the composition of the pigment; an infra-red light examination will reveal the middle layers of paint, and X-rays will expose the ground. Sculptures and assembled objects are also x-rayed, or even subjected to a CAT scan.

However, forgers are also aware of the tools and knowledge available to science.

As demand has grown, the numbers of fakes and forgeries have risen in proportion. As early as the nineteen-fifties, statisticians at government institutes had discovered that about sixty percent of all the objects on the antiques market were not genuine. Today, experts believe that in some areas, such as glass, up to eighty percent of all objects on the market are fakes. For the market as a whole, twenty percent is a commonly accepted figure. According to the EU authorities in Brussels, trade in art forgeries has been the second-largest illegal market, after the drug trade, since the early nineteen-nineties.

Various Kinds of Forgeries

The main characteristic of a forgery is that it was not made by the hand of the artist to whom it is attributed, either outright or by implication—i.e., it is not "original." A fake fulfills the desires of the art market. Thus, old works of art are forged so that they mirror the way that the artist is understood by the forger's contemporaries; current tastes and styles link the forger to his contemporary recipients. In this respect, the fake outdoes the original in its sense of closeness to the period in which it was produced. This is why many forgeries are not recognized until after a generation has passed; the succeeding generation is surprised that no one recognized the forgery for such a long time.

A forgery can be a direct copy, an imitation of a certain style, or a pastiche of single elements. Cases in which authentic works of middling quality are officially attributed to famous artists are not classified as forgeries; since these pieces are judged after the fact, without their material substance having been altered in any way, they are only false attributions.

The most frequently occurring form of forgery is the identical or modified copy of an original, created with a willful intention to deceive. These fakes are often accompanied by an invented provenance and faked exhibition labels on the back. A more refined type, however, involves imitating a certain style or special work method, without including specific elements of a particular work, and subsequently adding a fake signature or manufacturer's mark. Other ways to do this include imitating an existing piece using a different kind of material, or combining different parts of various works into a so-called pastiche.

But also authentic works of art that have been altered at a later date, with intent to deceive, are forgeries. Alterations—which can be done by a restorer, for example—include such things as painting over an older painting or adding a new element, which then affects the value of the piece.

Such alterations are only forgeries if an addition alters the entire character of a piece, and/or creates a basis for its market value—adding a signature is an example of this. Historicist wardrobes are gladly turned into Biedermeier wardrobes by removing the ornamentation from a baluster and adding ebonized pilasters; Biedermeier wardrobes are turned into vitrines by replacing wooden insets with glass. Generally speaking, old models can be used to create new molds for furniture mounts, which can be cast and then gilded to increase the value. White porcelain is painted and (slightly) re-burned, silver and glass are re-engraved or re-cut—the list goes on and on. In the future, the art market will be surprised by the products of computers programmed to reproduce the brushstroke of an artist.

Sales of Forgeries

Generally speaking, in order to avoid complications, forgers prefer to fake works by deceased artists in the middle price segment, because the complex examinations of higher-priced goods are not worthwhile to a forger. Also, many cases are never prosecuted in court, even if the deceived buyer discovers the fraud, because the buyer is responsible for proving that the work is a fake in order to be able to reverse the transaction—a complicated, expensive process that is best avoided if the object "only" belongs in the middle price segment.

In the field of fine arts, this is mainly true of works on paper, which are made with ingredients that are difficult to date. Selecting an epoch for a possible forgery, then, is dependent on the age of the paper that the forger is able to obtain; as a rule, fake studies of existing paintings are most often forged. These "smaller" fakes cater to everyone's interests: they minimize the forger's risk, the seller is released de facto from his obligation to act in good faith, and the inexperienced bargain hunter is lured in by the item. Classified ads, listed under "Art Trade" in the large daily newspapers, seem to be a good place to offer forgeries.

For a forger, selling something through an auction is, in theory, an almost ideal scenario. The advantage is that his forgeries appear alongside authentic objects, in the apparently serious atmosphere of an art auction. Small auction houses in particular are in danger of being victimized by forgers, since they want to have the largest possible selection available for their buyers, without being able to employ specialists in every little subcategory. In this setting, a specialized dealership will have an obvious competitive advantage.

Related Fields of Art

Two branches of art must be distinguished from the illegal trade in forgeries: copies and Appropriation Art. Also, spreading rumors that a work is a fake can destroy the value of a work, regardless of the actual facts.

Appropriation Art is a strategy used by artists in the nineteen-eighties and nineties, who questioned the sacrosanct concept of the original through avowed plagiarism. Sherrie Levine, Louise Lawler, and Richard Prince are among the postmodern artists employing this approach.

A copy that is acknowledged to be a copy and is marketed as one is also not a forgery; there is a large market that thrives on customers who want to decorate their domestic surroundings with masterpieces from art history, but who will not accept photomechanical copies. Big workshops, most of them in Southeast Asia, churn out "Mona Lisas" by the hundreds, in order to meet this demand.

Yet another recent development is the trade in "old" copies of artworks, which are sold as such. Until the nineteenth century, part of an artist's training entailed the study of techniques, by copying Old Masters, for example. Up until that time, there was a different notion of authenticity, as well as a more liberal relationship to the works of other artists; copying was not considered a lack of inventiveness, but proof of an artist's training and skill as a copyist.

In times when masterpieces are rarely seen on the market and are sold for astronomical prices if they do, "old" copies are regarded as decorative surrogates, and people like to buy them, especially if they are rendered in an outstanding manner. Auction houses have recognized this trend and stage auctions simply to sell copies of Old Masters, exclusively.

Negative rumors about individual pieces are problematic for both museums and the art market alike. Frequently, a whisper campaign, claiming that a certain piece is not genuine, is deliberately used to harm a museum director (who was in charge when the piece was acquired), or a private collector (who might want to sell a work). In the latter cases, the purpose of these kinds of whisper campaigns is usually to lower the price of the work, sometimes with the hope that the work might not sell at all—a frequent outcome, true to the motto *semper aliquid haeret,* or, "something always sticks."

Conclusion

Standards for measuring the value of a work on the art market are primarily based on the object itself or its artistic and art-historical value. Artistic quality, the execution of a work, its condition, its position in relation to rest of the artist's oeuvre, and the fame of the artist are the determining factors.

More and more, however, qualities that are either not inherent in the object, or other aspects of artistic and art-historical value are becoming considerably more important. Rarity, above all, is at the top of this list, but provenance and museum documentation are also gaining influence. If a work is well-known on the market and no longer fresh, it also no longer seems rare, and its chances of selling are reduced. This effect is reinforced by the increasing transparency provided by Internet databanks.

The idea of increasing an object's attraction by publicizing the fact that it was once owned by someone famous was, at first, a phenomenon of the nineteen-nineties. Mainly, this benefitted pieces that were already valuable and viable on the market. Other objects, which were otherwise unmarketable, could be sold in this way, though, too. Usually, however, these were not works of fine art, but rather, industrially manufactured products, and in the best cases, works of applied art. A work of art that is always in demand on the market does not need this kind of provenance as a foundation for its value; but such provenance can elevate a work's value, while attesting to its authenticity at the same time. This is also true of museum documentation, which acts as a neutral, opinion-making authority to reinforce the value of the piece.

In point of fact, the classic "oil painting" is still the art market's most important genre. However, a certain shift in interests is noticeable; demand develops and fluctuates dynamically, passing through one era to the next, going from movement to movement. In terms of value, the isolated position of the Impressionists shifted after the turn of the century, when twentieth-century works also began reaching the same price levels. Although sculpture has gained value in leaps and bounds, it still has not closed the price gap between itself and painting. Nonetheless, even in the field of sculpture, twentieth-century works still fetch the highest prices.

Likewise, after a long phase of undervaluation (in relation to newer art), Old Master paintings are now found on the annual lists of most expensive sales. There is also increased demand for Old Master drawings and prints, which are bought by collectors who can no longer afford the oil paintings.

For many collectors, contemporary art has become noticeably more accessible during the last twenty years, thanks to the activities of gallerists and museums, as well as media coverage and Internet information. Consequently, they became more willing to acquire these kinds of works at auctions, without the advice of a gallery, and the number of contemporary works sold at auctions has been on the rise ever since. To the degree that developing societies produce interesting art and wealthy social classes, the demand for art grows proportionately—both galleries and auction houses have experienced this, primarily with Chinese, Indian, and Russian art.

Applied art is mainly acquired for private, representative purposes; demand, therefore, is subject to stronger fluctuations and trends than the demand for fine art. Besides the growing consequence of pieces dating from the eighteenth century, most of the objects garnering higher prices were made in the twentieth century.

Along with the burgeoning interest in Old Master prints and drawings, the practice of dividing generalized auctions into smaller ones, where only particular types of art are sold, demonstrates that there is room for niche expansion. In certain narrow fields, dealers have an advantage, because they can offer individual pieces, while an auction house requires a critical mass of objects.

If certain segments of the market dry up, then the market looks for new fields, which can be subcategories or even a new medium from the same period.

Photography is an especially successful new field; it not only dominates a certain sector of the contemporary art market, but it has also replaced prints and engravings as the classic medium for young collectors. The development of sculpture into installation, or art into new media, however, is still marked by a certain insecurity stemming from problems of technology and the difficulty of proving the authenticity of a work.

New business opportunities have mainly arisen in areas where a famous provenance is the basis for an object's market value; this applies to the estates of stars, for instance. Pop culture products are also suited to the art market. The boundaries between these two fields fluctuate. Even though society is constantly producing celebrities, it is also clear that there is no inexhaustible source for memorabilia.

These new areas are primarily propagated by the big auction houses and presented via complicated client contact tools. Consequently, it is possible to realize prices that are clearly higher than prices on the primary market or those fetched by previous deals.

Today, the statute of limitations has expired for most old claims to looted art. Restitution, therefore, usually only occurs for moral and/or ethical reasons, and often under public pressure. This reduces the expectations for successful outcomes in cases against private owners, especially since the greater responsibility to exercise due diligence has resulted in the fact that no work appears on the market without being investigated beforehand.

To the art market, returned works of art are highly valuable, fresh objects with fully researched provenances, and this usually means that selling them generates a great deal of interest on the part of buyers and the media. Buyers also value these items because they acquire guaranteed, legal ownership of the work of art. In conducting this kind of business, however, the auction houses, as neutral middlemen, have a clear advantage over dealerships.

Market Supply

Managing Shortages on the Art Market

Normally, it is far more difficult to obtain wares of higher quality than it is to sell them. This situation is most obvious at art fairs. Due to a lack of good work, solo exhibitions, which used to make up the majority of displays at fairs, have become increasingly rare in recent years and have been replaced by group shows featuring individual works. In addition, desirable early works are becoming rarer, and often galleries only have recourse to the late works by the artists they represent.

In auction catalogues, too, it is clear that the amount of "filler" is expanding; the gap between these items and the exceptional pieces, which are actually in demand, is widening. On the whole, too, there are fewer objects being auctioned. Even though both Christie's and Sotheby's have seen profits rise, the total number of objects sold is about fifty percent less than what it was in the nineteen-nineties.

It is clear that the collector does not think of his collection in purely economic terms; he wants to keep his works of art, regardless of when it becomes optimal to sell. But why is it that objects are always "vanishing" from the market? First of all, pieces are damaged accidentally, in wars, or on purpose. Above all, though, if a work is sold or donated to a museum, it hits a dead end, as far as the market is concerned, since the majority of museums are generally not allowed to sell their inventory, or can do so only in exceptional cases.

There are different reasons why collectors' works wind up on the market again. Certainly, one reason is the need for money in emergency situations, such as when disputes arise among heirs, or in bankruptcy cases. The biggest private sources, however, are estate sales and auctions instigated by heirs. Here, too, the greater amount of information available about current market prices means that inexpensive purchases are becoming rarer, since the dealer's advantage, in terms of knowledge, is continually shrinking. Another motive for selling works of art is to rid a collection of erroneous or double acquisitions, or works of lesser quality.

If collectors decide to winnow out their collections, they can offer unwanted pieces to auction houses or dealers, or trade them in for a different work. Dealers are always interested in repurchasing works they have sold—they need it in order to cater to clients who want to add earlier works to their collections. If a dealer does not or cannot buy an object, he can take it on commission, which means that he acts as a middleman between potential buyers and the seller, who remains the owner of the piece until it is sold. In the main, galleries prefer to secure buy-back rights as part of the initial purchase, and will add a contractual clause that gives them the right to be the first to buy back the piece; should the collector want to sell the work again, he must first offer it to the gallery from which he acquired it. This means that as soon as individual pieces appear on the secondary market, the gallery has more control over the work than does the artist it represents, putting the gallery in a position to prevent speculation. These buyers' rights are controversial and especially problematic if the artist has changed galleries in the meantime, or if the value of the work has risen considerably. In the latter case, at least, the primary market gallery can try to hinder speculation by raising gallery prices when auction prices go to record highs.

When an artist dies, there is also more movement in the market. Sometimes bigger batches of works are sold in order to pay inheritance taxes. Media coverage and retrospectives focus public interest on the artist, and the oeuvre itself may undergo reevaluation.

A general problem with supply is that a kind of "cultural pessimism" has spread among younger collectors. Whereas before, the old was replaced by the new without a second thought, today there is a marked, basic conservatism. This younger generation of collectors can be contrasted with the "middle" generation of forty- to fifty-five year olds, who can easily part with an inherited collection, keeping only a few memorable gems. What makes the difference here might be the significance of the collection. Average works tend to be sold off, while the famous, museum-quality collection may instill in the heirs the sort of cultural pessimism mentioned above. At any rate, if there is a mixture of quality, one usually tends to dispose of the quantity and keep the quality.

Competition for Supply

Dealers interested in buying and reselling must calculate the profit that they hope to make when appraising a piece. The great advantage for the seller is that a dealer can immediately recognize what an object will yield and, in the best-case scenario, will pay him off.

As a rule, the price for objects from estate sales will be set by the person handling the dissolution of the estate. However, if a dealer discovers a good piece of work in a private household, he can offer to buy it. Frequently, though, when private parties offer a dealer a piece, they will overestimate the value of their property—the so-called endowment effect, which economist Richard Thaler studied in 1980 in connection with industrially produced consumer goods, is also true of art and antiques. Unlike an auction, where the seller can hope that competition among bidders will result in a price that is in line with the market—in case the auction house specialist has erred in his estimate—the dealer can be unjustly accused of trying to increase his own profit. Here, a dealer's expertise and candor will help him to establish a trusting relationship with his clients.

It is easier to set a price for a buy-back, since the original price is known and any increase in value, if taken into consideration, can usually be calculated without difficulty.

Finally, art dealers have yet another supply source. Besides buying directly from the artist, or from private, commercial, and occasionally museum sources, dealers buy a great deal at auctions. Even though many galleries at first avoided this path, dealers, who work with the secondary market anyway, have traditionally regarded the auction as an inexpensive, uncomplicated source of supply. In the meantime, galleries have been joining in, so contemporary art has become an inevitable component of the auction business.

The larger number of private buyers attending auctions, however, means that dealers purchase fewer and fewer pieces. For dealers, this makes the situation doubly difficult: from the dealer's point of view, private buyers negatively influence the price level at auctions, and so the dealer is forced to buy more works from private parties. Competition from the auction houses, however, also complicates things, since sellers are often familiar with the track record of auction prices—meaning that they will either demand a higher price from the dealer or even send their art directly to the auction house.

When a work is taken to an auction house, the client establishes the reserve price for the piece. The auction house specialist contributes his advice, since he has an overview of the current market prices. His determination is based on benchmark prices set at previous auctions, which set standard prices for a limited amount of time. Consequently, the auction house determines the price, de facto. When very valuable works are involved, an agreement can be made to set the limit just before the auction occurs—in this way, the auction house can react to the interest (or lack thereof) of potential bidders, after the catalogue has been published and the object previewed.

Determining the reserve price is a sensitive affair. If it is too low, competitive bidding might make up the balance, but that often leads to particularly hard-nosed bidding—as long as the auction house has a large enough public. Otherwise, an individual bidder might be lucky enough to acquire an undervalued piece inexpensively, for lack of competition. If reserves are too high and estimates too aggressive, buyers can be easily turned off. An auction house prefers to set the reserve at a moderate, conservative amount, since this increases the likelihood that an object will sell and may stimulate some active bidding in the room.

At times, exceptions are made for complete collections; in these cases, the auctioneer and the seller can agree upon a "global reserve." Here, individual reserves are replaced by a total sum. The auctioneer can then set reserves for individual pieces during the auction itself, since only the global reserve has been contractually agreed. In this situation, the advantage is that individual lots can go either over or under the reserve, without endangering the global reserve. This usually results in an overall higher sales quota.

When the objects are consigned to the auction house, a contract is signed, detailing the conditions under which the firm will sell them. This contract establishes the amount of the commission. The consignment agreement becomes the basis for the auction, and so it has to cover not only the items and their estimates, but all other agreements. In particular, clauses regulating charges for catalogue illustrations, as well as marketing promises, will be part of that agreement.

Besides the fact that they can pay the seller immediately, dealers have two other advantages over the auction house: it is easier for them to specialize in one particular area, even to the point of doing reputable scientific research. Naturally, this advantage is relevant to sales of works, since a dealer who specializes is also a knowledgeable salesman. Furthermore, specialization can really be effective when making purchases, especially at auction. As a rule, auction houses are generalists, especially when it comes to the middle market.

Dealers' second great advantage is that they frequently have more time to devote to their field of expertise. Between taking deliveries and printing catalogues, there is often only a short period of time in which the auction house's specialist can investigate all of the objects. Often, specialized dealers are able to sell an object acquired at auction for a significantly higher price than they paid for it because they have had the time to conduct research and hence discover important background information, while the auction house simply does not have this kind of time.

Client Contact on the Supply Market

When it comes to supply, the art and antiques market is very different from other markets. Primarily, it is not so much the "know-how" of the dealer or the auctioneer, but his "know where," which gives him an advantage. Dealers and auction houses acquire this knowledge in various ways. Both sides will offer free consultations to owners, middlemen, or even insurance companies. Instruments for acquiring client contacts can be divided into direct means, such as sponsoring cultural events, or into indirect means, such as building a network of references. By continually reminding potential sellers of recent successful sales, auction houses and dealers hope to show clients that their firms are in a position either to get buyers to pay the best possible price for their goods, or else pay the best possible price for the goods themselves.

Communications Policies

Contacting interested parties is a way to maintain and build a network of references, but it is primarily useful for finding clients on the supply side (see p. 149 *Client Outreach on the Market*). Apart from public relations, communications help to shape a corporate identity, but they also affect the supply side. Dealers contact clients on the supply side mainly through advertisements in newspapers and magazines, and by setting up their own Web sites.

Client contact can also be established by offering potential vendors free valuations. Here, the dealer, especially one that specializes, can obtain a good overview of the market, since many collectors turn to the market when they need appraisals for their lucky finds. In addition, a valuation creates a personal relationship between an owner and a firm, which may turn out to be crucial in case the owner wants to sell at a later point in time.

Furthermore, it is very important for an art dealer to stay in contact with other experts in his or her field; for those art dealers who also own a gallery, valuable contacts can be found among artists—and not just those represented at the gallery—as well as dealers, museums, art societies, art critics, publishers, and so on.

Additionally, dealers are able to publicize their business through publications, mainly their sales catalogues, but they can also write and/or produce other publications on topics from their field of expertise: books, newspapers, magazines, portfolios, collectors' editions, special prints, or even catalogues raisonnés. Researching art objects is one of the core activities for those involved in the art market, and it is not rare for a dealer with great expertise in his or her field to know more than scholars in academia do. By scientifically investigating an area of expertise, a dealer can document his sphere of activity and his knowledge, while a program gallery can publicize the artists in its program. Frequently, the dealer's expertise and his intensive, direct exchanges with an artist can result in important, landmark publications.

Another way for a dealer to create client contacts is to collaborate with a museum, either as a lender of objects or, better, as an author of catalogue texts. Meanwhile, market players with journalistic skills will occasionally garner further attention for their firm by publishing articles on their field of expertise in magazines and newspapers.

Mergers

Growing competitive pressure leads to greater specialization, on one hand, but also to increased cooperation. Thus, buying very valuable pieces—especially during times of small profit margins—is very difficult. For this reason, dealers have been banding together since the late nineteenth century to make joint purchases, called *á-meta* transactions. Often this means that a few financially strong dealers can control an entire field of the market. This practice is becoming more important in the field of Old Masters, above all, since these dealers must also actually buy the pictures they sell, whereas galleries usually only work with contemporary works on commission.

Although this way of working makes it possible to acquire very costly pieces, it can also entail some grave disadvantages: the more dealers involved, the more expensive a piece will be for a collector, since everyone wants to earn something from the sale. Also, these kinds of cooperatives give the participants a false sense of security, which hinders the individual's own initiative. Since the transaction must fulfill multiple obligations, these cooperatives only make safe purchases, which in turn hampers the dealer's job of discovering and promoting unknown artists or movements.

The Boundaries between the Primary and Secondary Markets: Gallery–Artist

Investment income that can only be realized through certain relationships, such as that between a gallery and an artist, is called quasi-rent. In such cases, the financial benefit is a yield that results exclusively through the connection to a particular partner. In order to secure their respective parts, the participants form a coalition in which they agree to do anything to guarantee each other's quasi-rent—or to refrain from doing anything that would endanger it. The gallery shows the artist's works in order to introduce the artist and his or her work to a larger audience and create a market for the work. At the same time the gallerist's selection of artists can provide the gallery with a unique profile, although in recent years, it seems that the larger galleries have tried to appeal to the broadest possible spectrum by offering potential buyers a very wide array of artistic directions.

The gallery signs a contract with "its" artists—or, at least, it should do so. Selling art on the primary market assumes a trusting relationship, which many galleries do not want to vitiate by requiring written contracts. However, even an oral agreement can be a contract and form the basis for rights and obligations. If a contract is agreed upon, the gallery generally has the right to lay out the terms, since it is obligated to give complete payment in advance. In this situation, there are several possible legal forms: artist and gallery can form a joint venture, or sign an agent's contract. These fundamental contracts include all of the rights to show and sell the artist's work as it is produced: it regulates minimum production of the work, the number of exhibitions, the rights to reproduce the work, the gallery's obligation to insure the warehouse, any of the gallery's possible claims to exclusive representation, and the division of sales revenue, in case the gallery only takes the artist's work on commission. If the dealer reduces the price of a sale, then the difference is deducted from his share. If the gallery buys works of art, the price of a work is, as a rule, fixed according to its size. If the gallery turns over any work to a subcontracted gallery, then that too must be regulated. If there is a licensing agreement, the gallery can also have the right to use and exploit works according to copyright law.

The dissolution of the relationship must also be regulated, because the relationship between a gallery and an artist is not always smooth. Some artists are persuaded to switch to a larger, more important international gallery as soon as they have established their presence on the market. Often, galleries lure promising artists away from other galleries; generally, they do this by promising the artist better representation, more professional marketing, and a division of revenue that is more advantageous to the artist. By the same token, galleries will stop representing artists who do not perform as expected on the market. In this situation, the contract must limit liability, in case one of the contractual partners takes steps that could damage the other, or the joint venture.

If a relationship between a gallery and an artist ends like this, there are often subsequent disagreements. The main issue is the ownership of the works that have been consigned to the gallery. Sometimes, after a contract is dissolved, completed transactions are examined more precisely and recalculations are made. At this point, it frequently comes to light that the relationship between the gallery and the artist involves far more than just plain business—for instance, when the gallery compiles an inventory, catalogues works, or prepares taxes or even a will for the artist. Generally speaking, it is obvious that relationships of this type do not last as long as they once did. Before, only a few artists who enjoyed great success around the world were represented by more than one gallery, but nowadays, this is good form in the globalized world. However, this also means that there is no longer just one person organizing the financial side of an artist's work. Artists have used this development to recapture some control over their market, which originally lay entirely in the hands of the galleries. The result is that some artists are now represented by independent agents, or even market their works almost completely on their own. Damien Hirst brought the concept of the producer's gallery into the twenty-first century. When it comes to purchasing directly from the artist's studio, the gallery is no longer the sole player. In the meantime, even the auction houses are going after the gallery's suppliers, meaning that they are also approaching artists directly, in order to obtain items. On the one hand, auction houses are used by collectors (see p. 45 *The Dealer-Collector*), but on the other, they themselves are going straight to artists, in order to make it possible to market new areas internationally. This happened and is still happening primarily with contemporary Chinese art, although, however, it should be noted that the system of primary and secondary markets is unknown in Asia, where all galleries hold auctions, and most of the auction houses also operate galleries. It is therefore not very surprising that artists from these cultural regions were the first to take their works directly to auctions, bypassing the galleries on the primary market. Damien Hirst's auction in 2008, where he provided his own goods, showed that some artists can take the liberty of choosing their own marketing channels, without having to consider old relationships or traditions. Still, this type of auction will probably have few imitators, for after all in order to succeed one must have penetrated international markets to a certain degree, and there has to be a great demand as well.

Auction Houses

In contrast to dealers, an auction house has an advantage on the supply side: it can promise a transparent process for establishing prices. If they are higher than the pre-sale estimate, the profit will be on the vendor's rather than on the dealer's side.

Consulting and References

Just as dealers do, auction houses also offer valuations in specialized areas; at regular intervals the big houses send experts to all of their affiliates in order to appraise items that have been offered.

For auction houses, though, references make up their primary instrument for acquiring contacts. A firm that has established itself in the mind of the client as a successful sales entity will receive regular requests for appraisals—the first step in consigning objects. In order to maintain this network of references, therefore, auction houses always publicize record prices.

Independent of these specific records, a list of the ten highest prices of the year is published annually. These tend to be made by the two large houses, Christie's and Sotheby's. There is also a list of the ten most expensive paintings of all time, although it is not regularly publicized. Instead, it is published when a picture is given a new ranking on the list—something that happened twice in 2010 (see p. 26 *Cartels and Globalization*). Each company also lists sales prices in its own publications, either in monthly magazines and brochures that announce upcoming auctions and that report on record prices, or in end-of-season or end-of-year reviews, some of which can be impressively elaborate.

Networks of references, however, not only make it possible for smaller firms to draw attention to the high sales prices they have achieved, but they enable firms to indicate their areas of specialization to clients. This can mean that the highest prices in certain areas or for certain artists are not attained by the international auction houses, but by smaller, national, or even regional firms. For dealerships, though, the pervasive media presence of auction houses, especially the big ones, poses a danger, because over time, the public gradually comes to believe that art is "normally" sold at auction.

Guarantees

One of the straightforward instruments utilized mainly by owners of particularly expensive objects is the guarantee. Big auction houses will guarantee a minimum sales price to owners of especially important pieces, in order to persuade them to consign the work. When it comes to guarantees, then, the financially powerful multinationals have an advantage over their smaller competitors. Although in Europe the guarantee has long been a business secret, American auction regulations require every auctioneer to mark in the catalogue all of the lots in which it has a financial interest, either in the role of owner or as the guarantor of a minimum sales price.

However, the seller should ask himself if it is really worth it to get a guarantee. If an auction house gives a guarantee, it takes on most of the risk involved in the sale, but the client must also pay for it. A portion of the sales price that exceeds the guaranteed sum belongs to the auction house. If the auction is successful, the seller only benefits somewhat from it, and therefore if the sales price is particularly high, the seller might not fully enjoy it.

Besides the financial loss suffered by the auction house when an object sells for less than the guaranteed price, there is yet another disadvantage to the auction house when it promises a guarantee. If the work does not sell at all, then it belongs to the firm; the latter can either warehouse the work—an expensive option, as it will certainly not sell until some time has gone by—or sell it at a loss. There is another alternative that is occasionally employed if the auction house does not want to guarantee the work: a third-party guarantee. In this case, an outside third party is the guarantor, not the auction house. After guarantees reached an apex in the two-thousands, the crises of 2008–09 led auction houses to promise them only if very strict requirements are met, and this has resulted in a massive reduction in the number of guarantees overall.

Other Financial Services

The big auction houses do more than just occasionally guarantee the price of a work of art in the hopes of seeing it consigned to them for sale. When Alfred Taubman took over Sotheby's, the company also began utilizing modern management techniques and offering financial services, too. For example, in 1984, Taubman began offering advances on the proceeds of sales, which could satisfy the immediate financial needs of the seller. As a rule, the advance is a maximum of fifty percent of the expected revenue, and the vendor must pay interest on this sum. In this sense, the auction house is providing a loan, with the work of art as security.

This has obviously been a crucial step in the competition with dealers, since the dealer's ability to immediately pay for an object has always been one of the great advantages of doing business with a dealer. At the same time, this was evidence that works of art are bankable—the foundation for further developments in art investing. In the meantime, all of the big auction houses are now offering advances of this kind.

Another instrument on the supply side is the middleman's introductory commission. Anyone who arranges the consignment of an object to one of the auction houses receives a commission when the object is sold; this commission is usually between one third and forty percent of the vendor's commission.

The Network

Since the nineteen-fifties the large auction houses have been opening branches, so-called representatives. In less than thirty years, they have not only expanded to the United States, but they have also created a global network of auction houses and representative offices, which makes it possible for them to react to changes in the art market and national (commodities) trends just as quickly as other companies in other branches. Even the smaller, regional auction houses are now operating branches or have hired representatives; occasionally, they are even represented by local art dealers.

A representative not only provides assistance with the administrative side of appraisals, consignments, or purchases, he or she also provides the firm with an actual presence on a regional art scene—a factor that not only provides opportunities to carry on interesting exchanges with local collectors, but also creates trustworthy relationships. The spectrum ranges from representatives who, after ending their regular work day, consult with clients and take on smaller consignments, to the representative offices whose staff do valuations in their own premises and will also arrange any consignments that may ensue. Other representatives carry out their own auctions, but take on objects for other firms on the side.

In countries where these auction houses do not maintain any auction rooms, the expense of transporting a piece abroad dictates the minimum price that the piece has to sell for, in order to even consider auctioning the piece. All of these branches, though, have to turn a profit; during financial crises especially, the network can shrink within just a few months, leaving only the truly profitable branches.

Relationships to so-called multipliers are also part of the network. These are people who either have contacts to potential clients and actually represent the house, or else are famed for their knowledge of art and the market. The latter, especially, are important to auction houses, which try to win them over by appointing them to a board that has no executive function, but acts in a solely advisory capacity. Alfred Taubman can probably be credited with inventing this method, because shortly after he took over Sotheby's, he established this type of advisory board and was able to persuade numerous collectors or aristocrats, such as Giovanni Agnelli and Heinrich Thyssen-Bornemisza, to sit on the board. Others followed his example: on the

Phillips advisory board, for example, are Francesca von Habsburg, the daughter of Heinrich Thyssen-Bornemisza, and Princess Gloria von Thurn und Taxis, as well as the photographer Jürgen Teller and fashion designer Marc Jacobs.

Another way to bind these kinds of people to an auction house is to offer them honorary chairmanships or presidencies. None of these personages has any executive function; their primary task is to maintain contacts. The fact that their names are particularly familiar to large portions of the population is certainly an advantage here.

Conclusion

In recent years, it has become far more difficult to obtain commodities to sell. On one hand, the general shortage of artworks has made owners visibly more reluctant to part with their property. On the other hand, informational sources, such as exhibition catalogues and catalogues raisonnés, have become significantly more discreet about identifying owners of artworks.

Dealers have an advantage in their ability to make direct purchases, since the seller is paid immediately. However, auctions are also an important source of commodities for dealers. Here, the situation has decidedly changed in recent years, since the growing number of private buyers at auctions can cause price levels to rise, while on the other hand these private clients will, in turn, supply auctions with objects to sell. Still, as a rule, the dealer has more time than the auction house to research objects. If he has acquired an object, his chances of discovering something in his research that will have a positive effect on the object's market value are greater. He can factor this possibility into his offer to the seller.

Both dealers and auction houses have access to the same kinds of communications; contact to collectors, external experts, museums, and other "multipliers" is key. Due to increased media presence, the corporate identity of an auction house, as well as its policies in dealing with references, can greatly influence the supply side of the market.

Auction houses can compete with dealers who pay up front for goods by offering similar financial services, such as advances and guarantees. However, since 2008–09, far fewer guarantees have been offered. As a result, guarantees have become extremely rare, and are only given to outstanding works of art that are new to the market.

The only way for dealers to establish a monopoly is to specialize in a certain area, or to limit their trade to a particular field. On the primary market, dealers can secure their position on the supply side by dictating advantageous terms in artists' contracts. In competing with the auction houses' networks, dealers can only balance out financial or administrative disadvantages by forming joint ventures and making *á-meta* transactions. These methods can be dangerous, however, because over the long run, they can dampen individual initiative.

The Sales Market

Dealer Sales

From the buyer's perspective, an art dealership is a mechanism of selection. Dealers sift through the offerings on the art market (whereas galleries go straight to the primary source) and select the commodities that fulfill their standards of quality and taste, so they are able to offer their clientele a "pre-selected" array of goods. This introduces costs that are ultimately paid for by the buyer: expenses for visits to art fairs and studios, for tracking the market and the competition, et cetera. As an end buyer, buying through a dealer also means that one has to trust the abilities and taste of the dealer; many clients are happy to accept the fact that these services come at a price.

A dealer has to appraise a piece he or she has acquired, beginning with an investigation of its neutral market value. However, all it takes is one client who is ready to pay the price asked, and this estimate can be exceeded—for instance, when the object fits perfectly into an existing collection or a particular space. A dealer can make a successful sale simply by offering the right pieces to the right clients.

Showrooms

A dealer has to present the objects he wants to sell in an appropriate manner. This means he has to take certain measures, such as having an artwork expertly restored or framed, but above all, the environment in which the work is presented must be right. A dealer sells in his showroom—his gallery—which is usually at street level so that it can easily be found by his regular clientele, while also attracting the attention of passersby with its display windows. Since, however, many important collectors of objects that start at a certain price or level of quality no longer make spontaneous purchases, a growing number of dealers only sell at art fairs, where they can count on meeting with motivated buyers. This is also true of upper-floor galleries, although in their showrooms these galleries ensure their clientele a certain amount of discretion, since there are no shop windows for the casual passerby to see through. From the more private upper-floor gallery, it is, then, just a small step to begin actually conducting sales "at home." The dealer's living room can be quickly redecorated, and every object placed there is offered for sale. Invitations to the opening are addressed to all regular clients as well as other interested parties they recommend. Afterward, viewing and buying objects can be done only by appointment.

Classic gallery spaces have the traditional white walls and light-colored concrete or wooden floors. More and more, however, they are being designed like private spaces, in order to present the gallery as a continuation of salon culture, where events such as readings or concerts can be staged—a concept that has proved successful since the end of the nineteenth century. Generally speaking, the better the quality of the artworks, the more elaborate and expensive the décor of the various showrooms, especially when it comes to Old Master paintings and the applied arts. Entire rooms can be decorated to represent different eras, in order to establish an aesthetic and art-historical context for the works.

In order to have their neighborhood work to their benefit, dealers typically locate their showrooms in close proximity to each other, which means that in every larger city there are neighborhoods where antiques dealers are concentrated. Likewise, there is usually a gallery quarter. More recently, art dealers have begun to cooperate with each other to found places for commercial art sales, such as a gallery complex—a set-up in which participants share some of the entrepreneurial risk. These places are especially buyer-friendly when they offer either educational or research opportunities in addition to commercial wares; instances of this are the Cologne Forum for Photography and Art, where there is a foundation for contemporary photography along with photography galleries, and the Swiss Foundation for Photography, which unites research, museum, and assistance under one roof.

Location

The art and antiques market is divided, meaning that sales opportunities and revenues differ from place to place. So location can also be a decisive factor in the success or failure of an art dealership. It is no wonder, then, that there can be a strong concentration of art dealerships in cities with high per capita incomes. For galleries, on the other hand, location is not necessarily as crucial. For one, they are more dependent on society's fundamental moods and trends than are dealers in Old Masters. For another, many galleries hope that if they have the right program, collectors of "their" artists will come to them, regardless of location.

The Network

A regional sales location can take the form of a branch or a partnership. Unlike the auction houses, where a network of representative offices primarily serves the supply line, dealers mainly use networks to support sales. Diverse large galleries have long had branches in important commercial centers. However, even without a local branch, a dealer can also access a foreign market. Dealers in a specialized area might work together, allowing each other to present one or more objects in a partner's showroom.

Art Fairs

In the postwar period, art and antiques fairs have taken on a great deal more importance, not least because they offer dealers a good opportunity to present their wares to a larger public in an environment in which they can also demonstrate their knowledge of art history. As time becomes increasingly precious, many collectors think of fairs as a way to obtain an overview of the market without spending too much time and effort. Fairs allow collectors to meet new dealers, and vice-versa. For galleries, in particular, a fair is an optimal way to publicize their programs.

Fairs are also a good opportunity to forge better ties to clients, since important collectors can be invited to previews before the official opening of the fair, giving them an exclusive chance to make purchases; Art Basel calls this kind of preview "First Choice." In Basel twenty percent of total admissions are paid at the opening night reception—which is only open to invited guests. Even for dealers who do not have stands, the first-class guest list means that they still have an outstanding place to meet clients and initiate business transactions.

Purchase patterns in recent years show that the world is not only experiencing the Internet age, but also the age of event marketing. A fair satisfies the consumer's urge for events. And indeed, for dealers, a fair is the only kind of sales event with an atmosphere that comes even close to the aura of a big auction. A fair's limited time period and accompanying program of events fuel the desire to consume. Special events range from the preview to combined presentations of artworks and antiques to displays of museum works on loan, seen as an instrument with which to "educate the eye." And, of course, the media resonance is significantly greater than in the case of an individual gallery exhibition.

For buyers, fairs also assure a certain level of quality, since the goods (or the exhibitor, at least) must meet the criteria required by the organizers of the fair. Each fair can only accommodate a small selection of applicants, who are chosen by committee. Still, the committees are unfortunately put together in a way that permits dealers to decide if other dealers will be allowed to exhibit. Also, exhibitors see Kunstvereine (art societies) and auction houses as competition and do not allow them to participate, either.

There are also drawbacks to the fairs' great public success: for one, the growing number of fairs has to some degree drained media attention and public interest away from the regular gallery world, even in the face of well-planned and artfully executed gallery shows. For another, prominent buyers might be scared off by the fuss and bustle generated by the increasing crowds of visitors. As a result, some dealers communicate to their clients that they are staying away from the fairs, in order to set themselves apart from the competition.

In the past, this kind of public success also meant that fairs grew in size—that is, the number of participants rose continually. It was not until the late nineteen-nineties, when the market was generally weak, that the financially weak operations were weeded out. As a result, almost all of the fairs lost exhibitors, but, on the other hand, they expanded their array of fields, frequently to include twentieth-century art, which was in demand. Last, but not least, this development drew the attention of younger collectors, who had formerly preferred to buy at auction. Ideally, fairs took advantage of smaller attendance numbers to sharpen their profiles and become easier to navigate.

Taking into consideration the admissions criteria, value, and quality of the works offered, the most important art fair is TEFAF (named after its organizer, The European Fine Art Foundation) in Maastricht, which focuses on Old Master and Modern art. Visitors regularly have an opportunity to enjoy more than a thousand Old Master paintings—

an estimated sixty to eighty percent of those available around the world are on the market here—and another five hundred nineteenth-century paintings. Modernist works are also becoming increasingly important. Altogether, around thirty thousand objects are normally for sale here, shown in elaborate, trend-setting ensembles and decorated with a plethora of flowers.

Art Basel, which has been held every year since 1969, is the most important fair for Modern and contemporary art. Every two years, it runs parallel to the Venice Biennale, which seems to trigger more sales, since many visitors attend both events back-to-back. Still, it is not only Art Basel's high ambitions and high sales figures that are indicative of its strong performance. In Basel, the organizers have tried to counter the sagging interest in large projects, such as video or other types of installations, by maintaining a special area, Art Unlimited, for which exhibitors are charged a reduced fee. There are also discounted fees for stands in the Art Statements sector, dedicated to up-and-coming participants. The fair has become even more attractive since 1996, when rejected applicants began gathering right next door for their own exhibit, the so-called Liste, which was later supplemented by other fairs on the side, such as the Volta Show. These events are not considered protests, but test stages, whose exhibitors ultimately aim to take part in Art Basel.

Art Basel has been so successful that an American version, Art Basel Miami Beach, was begun in December 2002. In this way, the organizers of Art Basel have successfully gained entry to markets in the United States and South America.

In the field of contemporary art, at least, Art Basel's biggest competitor since 2003 has been the Frieze Art Fair in London, which is organized by the magazine of the same name—it is quite common in other market segments for specialized magazines to organize trade fairs. *Frieze* employs its journalistic skills in an exemplary manner.

Even in the first year, the magazine's famous name, the glamour surrounding the event, and the fancy parties convinced many galleries to offer their works of art in the fall in London, instead of in Paris at the FIAC or in Cologne at Art Cologne.

Founded in 1967, Art Cologne features over two hundred galleries and garners well above fifty thousand in attendance numbers, making it the oldest and most important fair for Modern and contemporary art in Germany. In a kind of rebellion against Art Cologne, fourteen galleries united in 1996 to found the Art Forum Berlin, joining up with the Berlin Kunstherbst and its countless events. Art Forum Berlin is an emphatically youthful event, with particularly new works. Here, contemporary art is strictly up-to-date: only dwindling amounts of Modern art were on display in the beginning, and since 2003, only art produced in the second half of the twentieth century has been exhibited. Exhibitors also try to set themselves apart from the established competitors, not only by showing their works in tiny booths, but also by sometimes displaying their wares as a group, set up in generous-sized stands.

New ideas also come from the Far East, where the first non-gallery fair was launched in Shanghai in 2003—three hundred artists from around the world use it as a platform to show and sell their own works. However, the fairs in Hong Kong (ART HK, founded in 2008) and in Shanghai (ShContemporary, founded in 2007) are more meaningful to the market itself. The youngest European art fair—Multiplied: The Contemporary Editions Fair—offers prints and editions to a younger clientele. Held at the same time as the Frieze Art Fair in October, Multiplied was first launched in 2010, organized by Christie's in its space in South Kensington.

New Distribution Channels and Trade on the Internet

Ever since the boom came to an end in 2008–09, specializing in contemporary art has not only involved more effort, commitment, and risk, but the decline in business has demystified the whole trade. It seems that the classic professional gallery is retracting; due to the general increase in prices, almost no galleries can afford to maintain a large inventory, so only a few program galleries are still operating on the secondary market.

Often, even putting on an exhibition or taking part in a fair is regarded as superfluous; the goods are in the warehouse and are sold directly from there, without being exhibited—the dealer is becoming simply a broker. In order to be a broker, however, one must not only have the necessary expertise, but also excellent contacts to collectors and museums, which usually can be acquired only through years of working for an auction house or gallery. New media, communications, and distribution channels have facilitated and supported this development.

Art and the Internet seem to contradict each other in the same way that art and the market do: on one hand, there is the aura of the original and the role that it plays in the reception of a work, and on the other, there is the indirectness of media in the age of computers. In fact, some artists have always tried to avoid the art market by choosing to work with "ephemeral" materials. As the Internet has spread, Net art has arisen; it occurs exclusively on the Internet and it is not possible to market these works in the traditional way, by transferring ownership.

And thus, the significance of the Internet for art is not so much within the context of art reception; rather, it lies in its use as an informational and marketing instrument, as well as as a means of communication in the distribution process. Especially Web sites that document sales prices, such as artnet.com or artprice.com, have proved to be indispensible reference sources. These databases, which document auction prices, at least for works of fine art, continue to display this information for decades, and in turn, this has had a lasting effect on the art markets, by increasing transparency.

New media have, however, radically altered the image of art; art dealers can now publish Internet catalogues and open up Internet galleries. Interested parties can take virtual tours and make their purchases directly online. Even before Internet auctions were established, art dealers had discovered that the Internet could serve as a source of information, a presentational platform, and a distribution channel.

At least in the foreseeable future Internet publications will not replace the catalogue, though, because books can be picked up again and again, even years after the fact. Still, it is a way to open up art markets to a new generation of clients. Future generations of collectors may develop a completely different relationship to new media. Society as a whole is shifting away from traditional communications toward distance communications, and the lack of direct contact with commodities is no longer regarded as a great disadvantage.

Nevertheless, the art market is still an elite market, which limits its ability to earn yields on a massive scale. This can be seen in particular with the market for books, prints, manuscripts, and photography: in these areas, the fact that the Internet makes the market more transparent means that there is more competition among sellers, which can lead to lower profits overall. Naturally this affects mass-produced wares, because it is more difficult for the seller to calculate rarity into a sales price.

These problems, however, are countered by the great advantages of Internet trade. Market transparency is unsurpassed and almost every target group can be reached. Niche markets, in particular, have an easier time finding interested buyers. Before, anyone looking for specific objects or artists had to rely on a network of personal contacts, due to the strong fragmentation of supplies. Now, this research can be done much faster and more efficiently on the Internet. By using the Internet as an information medium, dealers have a chance to operate internationally without being tied to a location, and do not need the extensive, expensive network maintained by international auction houses.

Also, the first online fair, the VIP Art Fair, was held in January 2011. Although similar plans in the nineteen-nineties were not successful, the rapid development of animation and transmission technologies has made it easier to implement them. Animation technology today makes it possible to virtually stroll from one stand to the next. Individual works can be displayed in human proportions and enlarged, if necessary, while more surface details can be rendered through innovative technology. Among the founding members of this fair are famous galleries such as Gagosian, David Zwirner, White Cube, Hauser & Wirth, and Max Hetzler.

Client Outreach on the Market

In an ideal world, the art dealer would buy works of art, fill his showrooms and storeroom with them, and then wait for a buyer to come in and become enthused about an object. The classic example of this is the exhibition: a gallery will show the art of various artists in turn, trying to establish them on the market, while a dealer in works of the Old Masters will produce special exhibitions on particular themes or artists. Here, it is not just about putting works on display to edify the public—the show should arouse the visitor's desire to acquire and own this or that treasure. In addition, the dealer will be demonstrating his or her function as a caretaker of art. To this end, dealers will seek not just to have quality works, but also to present them well, very often in direct consultation with the artists. Also, there has been a recent trend to stimulate interest in commercial exhibitions by organizing a museum loan of works, which are not presented for sale. This is not just another sign of closer cooperation between dealers and museums and the blurring of traditional boundaries between the commercial and non-commercial art world. It is also a clever response to the market's increasingly short supply of valuable works. This is where dealers have an advantage over auction houses.

Today, dealers also energetically employ a wide range of tools for client outreach: advertising in all available media, and sponsoring cultural or even sports events. However, there is more to publicity work than just taking out ads; the art dealer has to state his program and expertise through the media, in order to engage in a public dialogue. To do this, marketers' publicity work must be on a professional level.

Another way to start an exchange with potential buyers is to create awareness by having receptions, summer festivals, and other types of parties. Special events on special topics are aimed at particular target groups; they are based on works in the dealer's current inventory, and experts in the field are invited to speak, so that the works can be explained to the guests. Finally, dealers will also devote events, such as parties for collectors or preview days, to up-and-coming artists. By taking certain measures, such as emphasizing works of art whose prices are below a particular level, or even producing entire fairs exclusively for affordable works of art, dealers try to reduce people's fears of embarking into the art world.

An important aspect of contacting clients is persuading them to visit the gallery. This is usually accomplished by holding special events, such as exhibitions, for limited periods of time, which suggests to the client that it would be particularly worthwhile to come visit during that time. Added value can be found in the show, the event, or even in a combination of the two.

Furthermore, firms can cooperate with each other on client outreach. This mainly involves engaging in activities such as collective advertising or collective exhibitions. Dealers who do not participate in fairs can still take advantage of the ones in their hometowns, putting on their own special shows in their showrooms and presenting additional events to attract those attending the fairs.

Apart from luring buyers with advertising and content, dealers traditionally offer financial incentives to get people to buy. As early as the first half of the twentieth century, Joseph Duveen was loaning pictures to his clients free of charge, or allowing them to defer payments for longer or shorter periods of time, without charging interest. Installment purchases are common today, and they give dealers yet another advantage over auction houses, where buyers must pay their bills in full immediately after the auction.

Word-of-mouth is another important way of contacting potential buyers of art or luxury goods in general. Cultivating a network of interested collectors who move in buyers' circles can result in more success than simply conducting a big advertising campaign. A dealer's outreach is more effective, the more targeted it is: what counts is how many potential buyers one contacts, not how many contacts are made in the absolute. In this case, there are no scattered losses to harm the marketing budget.

Catalogues

Like every other commercial branch, the art market also works with catalogues, which are sent to regular clients and are available at galleries. Here, there is a difference between catalogues produced by dealers in Old Masters and catalogues of gallery exhibitions. As a rule, when they are preparing their objects for sale, dealers in Old Masters can rely upon a large storehouse of art-historical literature about artists and their epochs. In contrast, gallery catalogues are not really sales instruments, but are generally the first critical, art-historical publication on the featured artist—a mobile communications tool used to explain the art.

Catalogues, written by experts and mostly illustrated, have always provided valuable and indispensible study material—not just for collectors, but also for art and cultural historians. They have an advantage over museum publications in that they cover a much wider range of objects. For dealerships, a catalogue is the best way to communicate their expertise and art-historical proficiency.

Transparencies, or large slides, are also important to dealers. They are often mailed along with catalogues, in order to provide even better-quality photos of valuable pieces and to put a work of art on display in several galleries at once, without exposing the work to the risk of damage and to save on shipping costs. In comparison, a relatively new advertising medium is the CD-ROM, which can show the current goods on offer with pictures and descriptions. Increasingly, it is replacing the transparency.

Lectures and Receptions

Lectures and discussions are particularly important in communicating art. For younger or unknown artists, this kind of communication can build a bridge between the canon of established art and the various forms of contemporary art.

Generally, the opening of a show at a gallery or dealership is a festive occasion. It gives galleries an opportunity to make direct contact with clients and to draw attention to new works. *Vernissage,* the French term for an opening, stems from the Parisian salons in the latter half of the nineteenth century. Originally, artists brought their works to the exhibition galleries, where they then added a protective coat of varnish; out of the French verb *vernisser* (to varnish) the noun *le vernissage* developed (lacquering; glazing; a preview). This was a day for artists to examine the works of their fellow competitors. The artist's friends and acquaintances, collectors, and critics also wanted to participate, and since 1900 at the latest the vernissage has been considered a social gathering for people to view a show before it is actually opened to the public. Soon it no longer mattered if the exhibition was held at a public museum, in a salon, at an auction house, or an art dealership.

If, at first, an invitation to a vernissage was a sign of social exclusivity, it rapidly lost its cachet, due to the increasing number of vernissages and visitors. Today, this means that particularly important clients have to be taken care of in different ways, sometimes by holding another, more exclusive pre-opening before the actual vernissage.

In the nineteen-nineties, museum education departments in several large European cities instituted the *Lange Nacht der Museen* ("Night of Museums" in the United Kingdom). On a specific weekend, all state-run museums are open all night. It was so successful that it attracted imitators, not just in other cities and towns, but also among dealers. Tours of galleries were started, or events such as *Die lange Nacht der Galerien* (literally, "the long night of galleries"). Occasionally, galleries in the same town cooperated to produce these events as season openers. On these days, showrooms are open longer than normal and frequently, a shuttle service takes visitors from one gallery to the next.

Special Events and Gallery Festivals

Many art dealerships hold special events when an art-related event is going on in the local city or region. The assumption is that an art-market event (for example, an auction of objects from an important field) or a cultural event (concert, festival, et cetera) will attract the type of public that dealers are also interested in.

It is now becoming more common for dealers to work with local auction houses on projects that go beyond buying and selling commodities. For example, exhibitions produced by galleries or dealers can serve as frames for large auctions. Sometimes these kinds of dealer shows can make up for the lack of a thematically related art fair—for instance in the area of Old Master drawings, where the two big fairs take place in New York and Paris *(Works on Paper* and *Salon du Dessin).* When the big auction houses in London hold their drawings auctions, eighteen dealers unite to set up a sizable show in their various showrooms, and the entire exhibition is documented in a catalogue they produce together *(Master Drawings London)*; this has been going on since 2001. At other times, dealers and auction houses will collaborate to create a new market segment, or to support an existing one; in this case, both parties organize and present sales and shows based on particular themes. The best example of this is definitely Asia Week, begun in 1996. During this week New York dealers, museums, and auctions focus their activities exclusively on Asian art, and are thus able to attract larger numbers of collectors specializing in this area. It has been so successful that a corresponding event was started in London in 1999, and Paris followed suit in 2001 with the Salon Internationale d'Art Asiatique.

Client Services

A great advantage for dealers is their ability to serve their clients, and the most crucial factor here is time. Clients have time to make up their minds about acquiring an object, since dealers will reserve works to offer to interested parties, who can pay later or in installments.

Before a purchase is made, the dealer provides consulting services. Ideally, he knows the interested party, is familiar with the collection, and can therefore give advice above and beyond basic information about the work under consideration. If a client is uncertain, then he or she can borrow the piece, and try setting it up or having it hung, in order to see the effect it has on its potential surroundings.

This kind of close relationship between a collector and a dealer can also mean that a dealer will comb the market for certain pieces sought by the collector. In recent years, dealers who specialize in doing this have had to expend considerably more energy: in the past collectors in individual fields bought items in order to build up their collections (and therefore acquired many objects over time), but a certain kind of eclectic collecting behavior has developed in the meantime, so that many clients only want to obtain a specific, outstanding piece in the field in which the dealer specializes. Hence, for every object sold, a great deal more research and background work is required.

When it comes to auctions, dealers can provide another service to their clients: large museums and collectors have always relied upon dealers to represent them at auctions, whenever they wished to purchase something and were afraid that their presence at an auction would drive prices higher.

Also, after a purchase is made, the dealer provides more services than does an auction house. As a rule, he will deliver the object, and then either hang it or set it up free of charge. He can often perform small repairs—a dealer's workshop frequently offers a range of services, from framing to expert restoration. And if a client is dissatisfied with a purchase, a dealer can generally be far more accommodating than an auction house. It is not just that he is liable for the characteristics of the commodity noted on the invoice. Most of the time he is prepared to take back an unwanted item or at least accept it as a trade-in for a new purchase.

The Auction Market

The Classic Auction

For centuries, the auction's fascinating, sensual aura and the ritual dramaturgy of what is basically an archaic competition have always resulted in moments in which participants hold their breath and even non-participants are enthralled: for many people, an auction is simply the most exciting type of event the art world has to offer.

The Auction Catalogue

The catalogue is one of the auction house's most important sales tools, and, as part of the process of building a network of references (see p. 129 *Communications Policies*), it also helps to attract consignors. Descriptions and pictures of the objects for sale are contained in the catalogue. Descriptions encompass all of the object's external characteristics, such as form, subject, frame, signatures, and condition, as well as information not actually embodied in the piece itself, such as its estimated value, ascription, or provenance.

Catalogue descriptions are only there to help clients with their purchases; they are not promises or guarantees. This can be found in the general terms and conditions of business by which all auction houses operate. This kind of limited liability clause has been declared legal by high courts around the world, because, for one, the auctioneer is merely offering consigned commodities, and is therefore dependent on the information provided by third parties, for example, the expert opinion in a catalogue raisonné. For another, people attending these kinds of auctions can count upon seeing this type of disclaimer printed in a highly visible place in the catalogue. In addition, an auction offers goods that have been previously owned—the sale of "used items" is legally regulated in a simpler way. The liability disclaimer is not even limited by the auction house's due diligence toward the client, as long as it can prove that the catalogue description is accurate, to the best of its knowledge and belief. A few international houses, however, will normally accommodate a client by taking back a piece up to five years after a purchase, if it has been proved wrongly catalogued in the meantime.

When it comes to attributions, catalogues employ a language of their own. A painting is only the work of a master's hand (in the opinion of the responsible specialist) if his full name is noted in the catalogue description. If the specialist is uncertain, he describes the work as "attributed to" the artist, meaning that he believes that part or all of the work was done by the hand of the artist. "Workshop of . . ." means that the painting was made in the artist's workshop during his lifetime, but not necessarily under his supervision. "Circle of . . ." describes a work that was also executed during the artist's lifetime, or at least during his era, and also shows his influence. "Follower of . . ." does not designate a student of the artist, but rather, some other painter, who simply works in the style of the artist in question. If the work is merely described as "in the style of . . ." then a long period of time has passed between the lifetime of the painter whose style is being imitated and that of the artist who actually painted the picture.

Primarily because of the interdisciplinary nature of auctions today, catalogues have changed their appearance. They are more colorful, for one, meaning, that the pictures of items on sale are printed with the four-color process. For another, the list of lots is broken up by staged photos of pieces from particular epochs, which also improve the visual experience. Some catalogues resemble expensive lifestyle or décor magazines.

In general, the provenance of each piece is given generous space, especially if it involves a famous person or aristocratic family, since that intensifies the desire to buy (see p. 79 *Provenance*). International houses use phrases such as "Property of a Lady," "From a Private

Collection," and so on, to denote items that come directly from a private party, not simply from a dealer. Since the market places increased emphasis on fresh commodities, these kinds of "Property Titles" are becoming more important, as is provenance information, since these references to private consignors can create a stronger incentive to buy. For family or tax reasons, however, many private collectors prefer to remain anonymous, and so the catalogue often has to outline a description of the collection without explicitly mentioning the collector's name.

As far as the quality of the objects for sale is concerned, their estimated value in the catalogue is significantly more definitive. Of course, the reserve price is the most important figure in the auction, since the hammer cannot fall until it has been reached. The catalogue, however, provides an estimated value, which sets the upper and lower estimate. For the international houses, the rule of thumb is that the reserve price should amount to about eighty percent of the low estimate. Still, this is just an approximate figure, and is frequently not applicable when it comes to important, coveted objects. Sotheby's first introduced the estimate in 1971, but nowadays it is part of every auction process. Prior to this, though, catalogues did not contain estimates. Clients were permitted to inquire after an estimate, but they were not allowed to make more than six inquiries per auction.

The estimate is a tried and true method of steering the bidding, since many clients recognize that it is a benchmark. Very rarely, an estimated price will not be printed in a catalogue; instead, the estimate will be provided "upon request." This is always the case when a piece is so rare and outstanding that it is impossible to appraise it, because there are no comparable items. Thus, information given orally might change as the number of inquiries from potential buyers rises.

The estimate of an object can contribute to its successful sale at auction. If it is set moderately, then more people are interested in bidding, which can create a lively, positive atmosphere in the room and, in the best case, result in a higher hammer price. Inversely, if an estimate is too high, buyers might be frightened away. Aggressive estimates conceal yet another risk: future consigners might also insist upon higher prices, even though they have already proved excessive. A consignor might nevertheless remain confident in the quality of his or her object and trust to luck. A rash of unrealistically high estimates would, however, cause an artificial bubble in the market.

Catalogues are sent to subscribers and consignors, as well as to collectors (unbidden and free of charge) who are known to be interested in the types of articles offered in specific auctions. Finally, catalogues are also used for cross-marketing: it is very likely that someone who acquires a work of Modern art will be interested in another kind of art, too. It is wholly possible that he employs similar standards in designing the rest of his environment and will seek out certain antiques or rare modern design objects for his surroundings. For this reason, an auction house will frequently advertise related auctions on the last pages of its catalogue.

The Preview

A preview does more than just provide clients a chance to examine the objects before an auction. The auction house is also a temporary museum, and for important auctions, presentations of goods are requiring more and more effort and expense. Over time, a complicated system entailing luxurious decorations and clever, staged previews has been established. Entire rooms full of items from a particular period are arranged, and interior decorators stage different scenarios, demonstrating, for example, how to integrate a collection of contemporary art into a room furnished with antiques. In addition, previews from various kinds of auctions are combined, to create the impression of "livable" spaces.

In terms of interior décor, the auction houses have long competed against the dealers for the role of trendsetter. Here they have an advantage, and not just because they start with more space and a bigger staff and budget. Since auction houses sell their goods faster, their presentations change more frequently than those of a dealer, who cannot finance that kind of outlay.

The Auction Process

The auctioneer begins by announcing the first lot, which is put on display, either physically or virtually. Bidding is done in ten percent increases; the person with the highest bid acquires the lot after the auctioneer has repeated the sum three times. Current bids are displayed on an electronic board, and they are also calculated in the most important international currencies—a practice instituted by German auctioneer Roman Norbert Ketterer, and quickly adopted by all of the big auction houses. The bid is not accepted when the hammer falls, but when the auctioneer says, "sold," "adjugé," "verkauft," et cetera. The fall of the hammer is simply an audible signal that the bidding is over, and the next lot can be announced; it gives the auction its rhythm. The hammer is also a kind of scepter, which the auctioneer uses to "consecrate" the bid and direct activity in the room.

Bidders in the auction room are recognizable by the so-called paddle they are given. These paddles are numbered, and no bidder can enter the room without a number so that the auction house can be sure of identifying buyers in the event of a successful bid. Bidding, however, is carried out through hand movements, and the more discreet they are, the more experienced the bidder. It is important to avoid showing potential competitors that one is bidding for the same piece as they are. The oft-heard rumor that one can unwittingly acquire a lot by absent-mindedly blinking or scratching one's head, however, has almost no truth to it—if there is the slightest doubt, an auctioneer will always make certain that a possible bidder is indeed actually bidding.

Consignors are forbidden by contract to bid in the auction, in order to prevent pushing bids on their old pieces. Every once in while, though, it does happen that a seller (sometimes through a representative) will bid and end up (inadvertently) acquiring the lot. In these cases, the auction houses are rigid and will demand that the consignor also pay the buyer's premium that they would have received from another bidder.

It is not until the final bid is accepted that the number of the successful bidder is announced. If there are no buyers, then the auctioneer says "passed." Particular etiquette is required of the audience at the moment the bid wins. It is absolutely taboo to turn around, in order to see who the buyer is. This is why the professional bidder sits in the back rows—he has already seen the objects during the preview, anyway, and so does not need to have a good view of the item in question.

The auctioneer initially announces the lot at about half the estimated value. This is supposed to stimulate potential buyers to outbid each other. Before the reserve price is reached, the auctioneer can also "bid to the chandelier." In this case, he simply calls out the next increment, without having actually received a specific bid. The auctioneer will often link this to a hand movement toward the room, in order to make the inexperienced part of the audience believe that a bid has come from the back of the hall. Sometimes this kind of bidding makes newcomers angry, since the auctioneer is simply pretending that there is an interested bidder for the lot. However, this practice can also be seen from the consignor's perspective: if the reserve price is not attained, the owner is not willing to sell the lot. Until the reserve price is reached, then, the consignor also effectively bids, in order to prevent the lot being sold at a lower price. Therefore, the auctioneer will bid to the chandelier on behalf of the owner. If the reserve is not reached, then the owner himself "buys" the piece.

For the auctioneer, it is imperative to stand "on the right foot"; this does not refer to the way he stands at the podium, but rather, to the correct bidding procedure. He knows the steps required to bump up the auction price of the lot. He also knows what the reserve is. If he has a written bid, then he has to measure the incremental increases so that the written bid can also win the lot, as long as there are no other higher bids coming from others in the room.

Now, if the reserve price is reached by the auctioneer's bidding to the chandelier, then procedure requires that there be an actual bid, too. If bidding in the hall ceases when the reserve is attained, but it has only been attained by a bid to the chandelier, then the lot is withdrawn, even though a bidder may indeed have been willing to pay the reserve price for the lot.

If there is a written bid, then the auction house is in an especially privileged position: it knows at what price the owner of the lot will sell, and what someone is willing to pay for it. In the age of telephone and Internet bidding, however, the written bid has, in general, lost some of its significance.

After the hammer comes down, the auctioneer is not actually allowed to take any more bids. If a client has made a mistake and wants to keep bidding, then it is very tempting to re-open the bidding, in order to obtain a higher price. Frequently, bidding on a lot will be re-opened much later during the auction. Therefore, the international houses follow the unwritten rule that "re-opening" is only permissible as long as the auctioneer has not yet announced the next lot.

"Bid spotters" have a very important task at large auctions. They observe the room and loudly catch the auctioneer's attention to be sure he does not miss a bid. Very generally speaking, about fifty to sixty lots per hour are announced; the slower the sales, the slower the auction, in order to give undecided bidders a chance to mull things over. On the other hand, long bidding wars can also slow down the whole process.

When famous dealers take part in an auction, it can be good for sales. Each bid submitted by these dealers is like a free appraisal of the object in question. If a dealer buys particularly important pieces at an auction, or pays especially high prices, his or her name is usually mentioned in the media reports. Not only does the publicity draw the attention of possible buyers, but a record price can often set a new price level for other works that may be in the dealer's warehouse. This kind of procedure, however, proves to the private buyer that he or she may be able to acquire a piece less expensively by buying it at auction directly. In order to solve this problem, a dealer will not actually bid for the pieces he or she wants to purchase, but instead, leaves the bidding to a middleman or else submits a written bid. The dealer's presence at an auction provides some glamour, however, which will later rub off on the object that has been anonymously acquired.

The Atmosphere

A good atmosphere contributes considerably to the success of an auction. First of all, this depends on the personality of the auctioneer, who not only has to be a master salesman, but a good entertainer, as well. An auction must engender curiosity and satisfy the human desire for sensation. The auctioneer's most important mood-related task is to generate the urge to buy, even coax forth the buyer's sense of possessiveness, in order to trigger competitive bidding. In some cases, it seems that clients are bidding simply because they really enjoy it. Many private collectors believe that it is important to have someone bidding against them. Not just because that makes them feel more secure in their choice, but also because an auction is a power struggle. Toward the end of a bidding competition, only two bidders remain. Each time either one stops to decide whether or not to keep bidding, the whole auction is briefly suspended, and the entire room holds its breath: this is a unique feeling of power.

It is clear that for many young people, exceptional experiences are a very special kind of luxury; it is no longer simply a question of "can I afford it?" as such, but also about the thrill. The struggle for a desirable object is a veritable battle that sometimes must be won at any price; it is a victory when the hammer falls in one's favor. The opponent could not keep up, has been beaten, and must once again prove himself. Nowhere else is so much money spent in such a brief period of time: the auction room is an outstanding stage on which to present oneself. By the way, American clients seem to be more susceptible to this nexus than is the European clientele—with the exception of Russian buyers, perhaps.

After the fall of the hammer, though, some triumphant buyers occasionally have the sobering feeling that they have paid too much—at the end of the day, no one else was prepared to bid as high. This feeling is called the "winner's curse." Here, the sole comfort is the thought that only the last bid was too high—after all, the loser was actually ready to spend almost as much.

If an object is especially expensive, or the bidding goes on for an especially long time, the victorious buyer is often honored with frenetic applause from the audience. Roman Norbert Ketterer, the auctioneer at the Stuttgart Kunstkabinett, rewarded the buyer in a special way: next to his podium stood a vase of white carnations, one of which he gave to each successful bidder.

Generally speaking, the atmosphere in an auction room thrives on the existence of a critical mass, which ensures the successful bidder the knowledge that his or her victory is a public one. From this point of view, the current tendency to sell more and more high-priced objects over the telephone can be regarded very critically: if this practice should intensify, then one day the eventful atmosphere of the auction room might be thrown into question, regardless of whether telephone bidding drives up prices in the same way that on-site bidding does. For the on-site bidder, the telephone bidder is no longer the obviously visible competitor, someone he can attempt to size up—in this case, as in the case of written bids, the public nature of the auction changes, taking on the aspect of a private transaction. It is unquestionably better for the atmosphere of the auction when the most important clients are sitting right there in the auction room. The significance of their presence is measured according to the probability of their bidding on the most important lots in the auction.

Seating reservations are usually distributed according to a plan, which is worked out with the help of a computer. By entering the name of a client requesting a reservation, a computer can immediately tell how much revenue this client provides, what kind of art he or she is interested in, what the client bids on, and how courageous he or she is during a bidding war. Naturally, the auctioneer knows the order of seating, so that when each lot comes up, he is aware of where the interested parties are sitting, and this also diminishes the danger of overlooking any bids.

Equally as important to the atmosphere in the auction room is the order in which the lots are presented; this is established by specialists in the field, who "compose" the auction. Only a specialist can assess a lot's chance of selling, and only he is familiar with the "problem cases." Important, critical, or especially expensive pieces are mixed into the lots whose chances of selling are high; this keeps the auction flowing, since a series of unsold lots can massively detract from the atmosphere in the room. Hence, the selection is always made to balance out the pieces that are good enough to make the auction as a whole seem attractive, with the affordable objects that will allow bidders who cannot afford the top lots a chance to satisfy their desire to acquire something. On the other hand, there should not be too many important pictures in one auction, so as not to split the interest of potential buyers. In large, momentous auctions, the pieces are divided into day and evening sales, and the more important objects are reserved for the evening. The selling off of the opening lot is always considered a good omen for an auction.

The Internet Auction

In the late nineteen-nineties, auction houses also discovered the Internet as the marketplace of the future. In the wake of the general success of Internet businesses and the stock market performance of Internet companies, a wave of companies dealing in Internet auctions followed. The basic idea was to use the bidding process to sell off the inventories of consumer goods in warehouses, for example. A company that wants to auction off its warehouse inventory over the Internet will design a website for this purpose ("business to people" sale).

Art auctions on the Internet, however, deviate from this model. First of all, every regular auction can be supplemented by an Internet event. Here, the events in the auction room are transmitted over the Internet, and Internet bids are taken in the same way that telephone bids are accepted. Early technical problems, such as occasionally lagging transmission, have been solved in the meantime. Bidders use a previously requested password to log onto the Internet site, provide their personal information, and can then see and hear the up-to-the-minute bids via the Internet; they can also bid with the click of the mouse, while the auction in the room comes to an end, as usual, with the fall of the hammer. On the other hand, a "real" Internet auction occurs when some of the lots are not offered in the auction hall, but only via the Internet.

Simply switching mediums is the easiest way for an art auction house to present an Internet auction. Here, the auction is prepared just as a regular auction would be, meaning that the in-house experts appraise the items, and then select and catalogue the appropriate objects for the auction. Only in-house specialists assemble the auction, appraise the goods, and prepare the catalogue texts. The house is liable for providing the correct information concerning attributions, ages, and conditions of each work, according to the normal liability framework. The catalogue is published on line, but not in print. The Internet replaces the physical event, the physically present bidders, and the telephone bids.

In spring 1999 a group of international auction houses and galleries operating under the name of International Auctioneers (IA) produced its first Internet auction, *Arts on Paper,* using the model described above. Large auction houses, such as Sotheby's and Christie's, at first rejected the idea of their companies presenting Internet auctions. It was not only because they doubted that they would reach the desirable "high-end clientele," but primarily because they were afraid that this kind of auction could have a negative effect on their revenue, since it was assumed that yields were essentially reliant upon the specific atmosphere in the auction room.

After a few test runs, Sotheby's gave up this attitude in mid-January 1999, and announced that they would begin holding their own Internet auctions that same year. They decided to employ the eBay model, a kind of Internet auction in which the vendor supplies the choice of objects and then presents it on the auction house website for a limited amount of time, usually one week, although it can be different for every field and every object; this is called a "rolling sale." This form of organization aims to use the opportunities offered by the Internet in a consistent manner, since, due to the different time zones, it is possible to reach more people with 24/7 offers than can be reached with a live event. Of all the bids that come in, the highest one is displayed on the home page. When the time is up, the object is sold to the highest bidder, who pays with a credit card. This payment, however, does not go to the auction house, but to the vendor. As soon as the latter receives the sum, he or she sends the object to the buyer and pays a commission to the auction house.

This procedure is highly advantageous for everyone involved: the pieces are catalogued, appraised, and photographed by the consignor. Consequently, the auction house specialist does not have to spend time on it. The object remains with the consignor, which saves the cost of transporting it to the auction site: when the house has to work on an object directly, it must be moved between five and ten times, generating additional costs. As a result, costs with Internet auctions are generally lower, meaning the auction house can charge a smaller commission. The consignor promises to store the wares for the length of the auction and not to offer them to anyone else. Everyone involved in the market can also rapidly acquire a precise overview of which kinds of goods are selling and where. Here, interesting synergies arise between Internet search systems and the internal databases of auction houses. Also, the vendor benefits from the fact that the auction houses widely advertise Internet auctions.

Sotheby's reworked and expanded its Internet concept before it was actually implemented. In June 1999 the company agreed to cooperate with Amazon.com, the Internet's biggest book dealer. Sotheby's primary interest here was in Amazon's ten million customers. However, these auctions soon proved that they would not achieve the projected revenue targets. After rather surprisingly breaking off the relationship with Amazon in 2001, Sotheby's at first began holding its own auctions, but then moved on to a direct association with eBay in July 2002. eBay was not only a pioneer in the field of Internet auctions, but it was also the global market leader and operated at a profit. Even so, it did not seem to be in a position to sell extremely valuable items or art objects; after just a few months, the "Great Collections" page was shut down. The alliance had not brought Sotheby's the amount of business it had hoped for, and so the entire Internet project came to an end in May 2003, after only a few weeks and hundreds of millions of dollars in losses.

Risks and Opportunities

Of course, one wonders why one of the biggest auction houses failed to this extent. Obviously, selling art via the Internet is riskier than expected; the effort and problems involved in online auctions should not be underestimated. For this reason, many businesses have started conducting auctions that sell only to dealers.

Up to now the biggest problem has indeed proved to be the uncertain economic return—on the art market, too, money is still mainly earned through the old economy. Costs for online services are very high; the producers have to manage all of the bids around the clock, in "real time," so 24-hour service is an imperative. Although eBay has a high rate of merchandise turnover, the company actually earns very little profit; even though this is not terribly unusual for an auction house, it is abnormal for a company that operates exclusively on the Internet. Twenty-four-hour service costs money, but does not make a considerable difference in the number of bidders: one of the prognosticated advantages of the rolling sale—the notion that round-the-clock service would balance out the global time differences—has not turned out as expected. Just before the end of a rolling sale, the number of bids rises drastically.

The problem with Internet auctions is that they mainly deal in inexpensive commodities. In 2000, the average price for a lot sold via Sothebys.com was $1,438, while the average price for a lot at a live auction was over $14,000. This confirms what could be seen merely by observing art-related Internet sales: the behavior of Internet shoppers is not compatible with the rather elitist art market. Thus, young people now make up the majority of buyers at Internet art auctions; before, they may never have bought anything at an auction but instead found what they wanted at secondhand dealers, markets, or fairs. For instance, even prior to the beginning of Internet auctions, secondhand books and prints were regarded as particularly good sellers on the Internet.

Security risks inherent in Internet transactions also manifest in Internet auctions. Especially for the consigner, the anonymity of the Internet can lead to disaster, if it turns out that a supposed client actually has no serious interest or is even a swindler, or if those involved in a transaction cannot be precisely identified. To protect their clients and provide security, auction houses have implemented their own security systems.

Despite these risks, an Internet auction can be a very good opportunity. Today, no less than one hundred and fifty auction houses hold Internet auctions, including famous art auction houses such as Christie's and Bonhams. Ten years after Internet auctions began, the "Christie's LIVE" model has proved the most successful. A Webcam broadcasts the auction on the Internet, and prospective buyers can watch and bid directly via their computers at home, as well as from laptops and all smartphones, from the iPhone to the Blackberry. This is more in line with the preferences and needs of the collector than a rolling sale is. Ever since Christie's introduced "Christie's LIVE," the Christie's Web site in general has had more than twice the number of visitors than the Sotheby's site receives. Obviously, the Internet auction also helps the auction house with its general communications and networking on the Internet, as well.

New Distribution Channels

One problem that auction houses in the top market segment experience is what to do when consigned pieces do not sell. If a piece has not sold at an auction, it is considered "burned," which essentially means that it is unsellable. This is where a large dealership has the advantage, since it can discreetly offer the piece to potential buyers and thus avoid public disgrace. International auction houses have based their counter-strategy on the expansion of their distribution channels, and hence, in the past, they have repeatedly bought galleries.

For instance, in 1996 Sotheby's purchased the André Emmerich Gallery and hired the former owner; in 1997 Sotheby's acquired fifty percent of Jeffrey Deitch's gallery. The Emmerich Gallery was closed in 1998, after Sotheby's had obtained access to the artists' estates managed by Emmerich, and established its own contacts to the living artists represented by the gallery. Another of Sotheby's acquisitions is Noortman Master Paintings in Amsterdam (purchased in 2007), a leading gallery for Old Masters, as well as nineteenth- and twentieth-century art. In 2006 Christie's bought Haunch of Venison, and thus acquired an international, primary market gallery with showrooms in London and New York. Yet, these kinds of networks can be found even in the middle market; for example, Michel Pastor, a co-owner of the French auction company Arcturiel-Briest-Poulain-F.Tajan, also has shares in the Gismondi and Marlborough galleries. Through this kind of acquisition, auction houses expect direct access to artists and their current productions, especially on their secondary market. Although the strategy seems to be mainly aimed at competing auction houses, and secondary market galleries in particular, it also contributes to more commercialization, which in turn has a stronger effect on the market in general.

The Battle for the Middle Market

As international houses have undergone restructuring in recent years, the focus has been on the so-called middle market, where commodities priced between roughly fifteen thousand and one hundred and fifty thousand dollars are sold. Servicing this market are countless firms located in European capitals, especially in economically important financial centers, even though they rarely have access to clients outside of the region or country. Thus far, it has not been possible to centralize the market in the way that the top segment is centered on London.

The differences between the middle market and the top market segments are very large. The most important factor is the lower average price for lots sold at these auctions. Therefore, overhead must be kept low, regardless of whether it is in the area of catalogue design or marketing.

There are several reasons why the top market segment is interested in the middle market. For one, about half of the objects in middle market auctions are bought by clients from the top segment. Therefore, these auctions are an appropriate means of finding clients and establishing loyalty. For another, commission and fee structures in this segment are particularly advantageous, from the standpoint of the auction houses, and can yield up to one-third of the sale price for the company. Also, the already high level of income is not reduced by expensive financial services, such as guarantees, which are limited to the top segment.

For over twenty-five years the Christie's South Kensington branch has demonstrated that solid profits can be earned even with less expensive pieces and unusual types of goods. Sotheby's first attempt to establish a comparable sales track failed in the nineteen-seventies. This smaller auction house, Sotheby's Belgravia, was located in London's Belgravia area, a very expensive, established neighborhood with very little foot traffic. Mayfair is a world away from the lively student and tourist district of South Kensington. At the time, Sotheby's idea was based on the notion that it was not enough to offer inexpensive goods in the usual categories. Unusual wares, collectibles, souvenirs, pop and sports articles can only be sold, however, if the auction is located in a place that does not intimidate the younger public. As of 2001 Sotheby's only involvement in the middle market entailed auctions held at Olympia, the fairgrounds in London, until this branch was also closed, after a six-year run. Subsequently, Sotheby's essentially withdrew from the middle market.

Bonhams, a classic middle market company, decided to take a different path. Founded in 1793 and family-owned ever since, Bonhams was eventually forced to acknowledge that it would be harder to survive independently than it would be to go into partnership with another firm. In 2000, a partner was found: Robert Brooks, which had developed from a shop for vintage cars in 1989 into one of the leading auctioneers of automobiles. The merger in 2000 created the fourth-largest auction house, Bonhams & Brooks, and the firm quickly expanded. In July 2001 Phillips agreed to merge with Bonhams & Brooks. The new Bonhams consisted of 50.1 percent of Bonhams & Brooks, and 49.9 percent of the smaller departments at Phillips, which belonged to LVMH at that point in time. The newly created Bonhams had its headquarters in the Bond Street showrooms once occupied by Phillips. After the biggest Phillips shareholder LVMH pulled out, Bonhams became the "third-largest auction house in the world," and to secure its position in summer 2002, it took over the most famous American auction company, Butterfield's, with locations in San Francisco and Los Angeles.

As the middle market was rediscovered, firms such as Bonhams and Christie's devoted their energies to this market segment in a more sustainable and even more professional manner. This market, which has shares worth fighting for, is not really international, like the top segment. Hence, these developments have ramifications for London or British competitors, rather than for European companies.

Client Outreach on the Sales Market

Auction houses highly value methods of acquiring client contacts on the market. Measured against the tradition of the auction house, this is a relatively new development. Originally, companies focused on acquiring consignments. When it came to sales, one could rely on the quality of the goods. Although today, in certain quality areas, acquisitions are still considered more difficult than sales—even taking the tough competition into consideration—there is still a preponderance of ways to secure them. This imbalance is so great that it can no longer be explained by claiming that "measures to promote sales are also measures to promote consignments," and then alluding to policies for building a network of references. Instead, the explanation has more to do with the fact that, through clever marketing, it is far easier to double the value of an Impressionist masterpiece than the results of a furniture or porcelain auction.

The Buyer's Premium

The reason for the increased activity in sales is that for more than twenty years, auction houses have earned more commission through sales than through acquiring consignments, since buyers also pay for the services of an auction house with a buyer's premium. This ranges from ten to twenty-five percent of the winning bid, depending on the actual price realized.

Sotheby's decided to introduce the premium in 1973. Prior to that, buyers did not pay any extra fees to purchase something at an auction; the auctioneer's income came from the vendor's commission. Just a few of the smaller houses on the European continent had already introduced the practice. Christie's followed on Sotheby's heels and introduced the buyer's premium that very same week.

This premium has had a lasting effect on the market; it has made it possible for the large houses to offer competitive vendor's commission rates, resulting in overall lower commission rates. The buyer's premium has had to compensate for that, though. Since the consignment market is relatively small, more sales have to be made in order to raise revenues. This is at the root of why the auction houses constantly put so much effort into acquiring private buyers.

Instruments

Relying on private buyers (those who are not aiming to re-sell their acquisitions and are thus in a position to bid higher than most dealers would) generally only pans out in the case of expensively staged auctions. These types of auctions mainly deal in top-quality goods, or items with important provenances, such as estate or castle auctions. As far as all other types of auctions are concerned, the level of prices realized is still lower than the prices dealers can get for objects.

Since the commodities offered by art auctioneers are not mass-produced products, marketing them is a very complex affair. Clever staging has a significant impact on the financial success of an auction. Depending on the notability of the objects or the consignor, proper advertising must be carefully timed and carried out.

Among the most important PR tools are ads in relevant magazines, as well as in international, inter-regional, and local newspapers. For a long time, auction houses have also made it a practice to sponsor cultural or sports events. Internet auction houses have their network providers advertise for them.

Another important PR tool is the auction calendar. There is a wide range of these publications, from calendars that report on the most notable auctions, to those that publish an assembly of various press releases, to simple lists of auction dates in chronological order. In art centers such as London, a few auction houses even publish monthly guides to all of the diverse kinds of art events: auctions, opening receptions, exhibitions, fairs, and the like.

An easier way to obtain an overview of objects and auctions is to employ the auction houses' computerized search engines. Here, collectors can enter their field of interest, and the firm will then notify them by letter or e-mail if a potentially interesting object is about to be auctioned.

On the auction houses' homepages, visitors can obtain information about available objects and services, as well as about the auction process itself. The regular catalogues for showroom auctions have been available online since the late nineteen-nineties, and the search engine is also on the homepage. Clients can receive e-mail reports on the conditions of various lots. Under development now are electronic consultants, which employ a client's user profile to help him search for the products he wants, and will also suggest items that might correspond to his preferences.

Before large auctions, firms will gladly send the objects on an exhibition tour. Stops are usually made in the major market cities or in a place where an outstanding work originated. For the companies that have headquarters in London and New York, exchanges are a way to reach clients on both continents; goods from the London auctions are shown in New York, and vice-versa. Besides simply presenting the objects, these types of shows give companies opportunities to approach clients at receptions, previews, et cetera, and invite them to develop a relationship with the firm.

A special kind of tour is undertaken to advertise jewelry auctions. Since jewelry is a classic fashion article, it is particularly important to put potential buyers in contact with the original objects. To do this, dinner parties are held for interested parties who wish to try on pieces before buying; first, the jewels are displayed in cases, and experts are invited to speak about the objects. Between courses, however, the various pieces of jewelry are handed around by employees of the auction house, so that guests can try them on.

Last-ditch efforts to sell an object are made when all other mechanisms and strategies have failed and the piece has not sold at auction. Aftersales give clients the chance to set their own bids for a lot. These aftersales are very important, financially speaking; in the case of some auctions, aftersales can move up to ten percent of the wares offered. According to their significance, the unsold objects in smaller houses will also be on display during the break between auctions. Many auction houses always have pieces on display, either for aftersale or as a lot in an upcoming auction, so that clients can preview objects and buy at almost the same time. This is a crucial element in competing with dealerships: clients do not have to worry about when they will attend an exhibition at an auction house. The auction house is a place where one can always find something, free of the auction schedule. Selling objects on a regular basis is just one aspect of the long-term planning for all houses. The eventful nature of the auction has to expand beyond the auction room itself, and so today, even bookshops, public catalogue archives, and restaurants assist in supporting the auction houses' sales efforts.

Client Services

Undertaking appraisals is the oldest service offered to clients. Beyond that, firms offer many different types of ongoing consulting and can even organize a client's entire participation in an auction, from making hotel reservations to framing the work acquired.

Consultation

Experts first do oral appraisals, and these are free of charge. The advantage for the auction house is that it now has direct contact to the owner, thanks to the personal contact between the collector and the expert. Once this has been established, the collector is more likely to return for advice regarding other pertinent matters.

To obtain a written appraisal, a client must pay the standard rate, which is based on the appraised value. If, prior to a "house sale," the contents of an entire house or castle has to be appraised, then the owner has to pay a fixed fee per day for every expert employed on the project. This is reckoned into the auction costs, if the consignor contracts to sell.

Auction houses also advise heirs how to deal with inherited works of art. Here, the issue is not just how much a work is worth and what would be the best way to sell it; the very specific organization of legal and tax advice might be included. These services are also extended to those who are advising the auction house's potential clients: attorneys, notaries, and estate and tax planners are among those who receive advice from auction houses. Consultation is also provided to insurance companies, since it does not pay for them to hire their own art experts.

In addition, auction houses try to familiarize potential clients with this initially unfamiliar distribution channel, known as the auction, while at the same time soothing their fears of the unknown. Many inexperienced clients are afraid that making a mistake in the auction room might have expensive consequences. To counteract this "auction phobia," Sotheby's has developed a three-step "New Collectors Program." First, new clients receive simply written, extensively illustrated brochures, in order to familiarize them with the objects in the auction. Then there is a theoretical introduction to the auction rules. Finally, clients are given the opportunity to visit an auction in the company of a guide, and then to analyze it afterward. By contrast, it has proved relatively easy to win over new buyers from Asia or the former Soviet republics: many of these collectors are entrepreneurs whose professions have made them familiar with the auction as a distribution system. Many commodities, especially raw materials or even services, are sold at auction, so some art auction novices already have a certain familiarity with this distribution process.

Organizational Assistance and Financial Services

Services pertaining directly to auctions include the organization of transportation for consignments or acquisitions; if need be, this is done by the firm's own shipping department. The company's own restoration and framing workshop offers other services; as a rule, consignments are not restored before an auction, since every restoration job raises questions that one would rather have answered according to the preferences and attitude of the collector or museum acquiring the piece. Also, private clients are advised as to how to conserve and store the works of art in their collections.

All of the large auction houses have their own credit departments, whose main task is to validate high bids, which are only accepted when a bank guarantees them. However, these departments also deal with extending payments. All auction houses require the purchase price to be paid in full immediately after the hammer falls. Almost all of the firms offer regular clients an installment option, called a 30-60-90, but the consignor must also agree to accept it, as well. The figures represent the intervals (in days) at which an installment is due. These rules are not only needed to help stimulate undecided buyers to bid, but it is just as likely that a bidder who is assured of an installment plan will drive up the final price, which is then paid immediately by the actual buyer.

There are other forms of credit available to dealers who make purchases and consign articles simultaneously. These financial arrangements are services provided by the houses, but they are also instruments that can be used to support both the acquisition of consignments and to engender sales. These are open credit loans, so that the objects can be taken away immediately. Generally, in between the time they purchase an item and the time the loan is due, dealers take advantage of these credits to re-sell the item at a profit.

Other Services

Rounding off the services offered by the big auction houses is education. In a broader sense, one could count internships as part of this area, for, after all, students are given a view of how business is done on the art market. The aura surrounding the auction increases the demand for internships, and consequently, the number of interns working at auction houses has risen dramatically.

Education in the traditional sense is offered by the firm's own institutions, where anyone can have access to the expertise of the auction house, for a fee. Courses range from simple night-school extension courses to workshops on specific topics, to complete art programs, which are affiliated with universities and award Master of Art degrees. Courses on diverse topics are also often covered by books authored by specialists in specific fields; many of these books are "collector's guides."

The various departments also hold lectures or conferences, which not only helps them make new contacts, but also provides outsiders with easier access to art. This is accomplished by organizing special museum tours, too, or presenting discussions with artists, instrument makers, artisans, restorers, and so on. Last, but not least, copyrighted photographs of auction items are marketed, or even loaned out as instructional material.

Furthermore, empty auction rooms are available for "non-commercial" exhibitions outside of the auction season—the so-called winter exhibitions in London. Here, contacts to collectors are used to find privately owned works of art and present them to the public; this also draws attention to the firm during the quiet winter season.

All of these services—most of which are subject to charges, by the way—are currently just bonuses in relation to the core business, and the auction houses expect that they will result in a clear premium in the near future. The auction houses' real estate divisions in particular have yielded high profits over the years. Yet, some services are offered free of charge, too. For charities in particular, auction houses are glad to provide their know-how and an auctioneer free of charge. However, a few prerequisites have to be fulfilled first: the purpose must be clearly charitable and serious, and the institution behind it must be a professional one.

Sales through a Hybrid of Dealership and Auction

The dealer who also works as an auctioneer is a somewhat frequent occurrence. Most art fairs refuse to allow these types of businesses to participate. This kind of association is problematic when it comes to the validity of their auction results. Each result can be unreliable: a so-called consignment might come from the dealer's own warehouse and is returned there after the auction, in the event that no buyer is found. Often, however, simply shifting the works of art around on paper is an accounting trick; these movements are noted as "sales" in order to statistically increase the auction's sales quota.

However, also falling into this category are private sales made by auction houses. Here, the auction house is trying to help a client who shies away from the public atmosphere of the auction room. Even though these kinds of sales have long been established, the media did not discuss the practice until Christie's and Sotheby's founded departments devoted solely to private sales, in order to professionalize the service. Since it is actually more important to the auction houses to find interesting objects for their own auctions, this service was only discreetly marketed and not advertised. Phillips does a great deal more in the area of private sales. Simon de Pury pitches his company's extensive private sales as an advantage over his competitors, which has, in turn, spurred competitors to publicize this service to a previously unheard-of extent.

Conclusion

In summary, there are a variety of challenges facing both dealers and auction houses with respect to sales. For dealers, the selective approach they employ to find artworks and offer them for sale results in higher costs. In many market segments this creates financial pressure that not only forces them to cut back on their methods of contacting clientele, but sometimes even leads them to give up their galleries or showrooms. Consequently, this turns dealerships into simple broker's offices.

The growing number of art fairs has increased competition among them; more effort must be made to win over important participants. The fairs that are successful are those that have created a profile for themselves at the right time and that continue to enforce strict quality standards and offer a wide array of goods. The art fair organizer has to have professional marketing and should not underestimate the allure of glamour and parties. In economically uncertain times, when twentieth-century art is particularly treasured, works from this period must be on offer. A large selection, however, should not come at the price of many exhibitors. Fairs offer dealers good opportunities to display not only their artworks, but also their expertise. If there is a lack of available objects, it is particularly obvious at fairs. This is the biggest danger of the "high-end" fairs.

Selling exclusively over the Internet is the exception for galleries and art dealers, and these types of sales are mostly made in the lower price segments. The Internet is an ideal informational medium and can therefore balance out two disadvantages of dealerships: being tied to a location and strong fragmentation. Thus, the Internet is an instrument that can be employed to win back private clients from auction houses. On the other hand, the Internet also intensifies competition among dealers.

Increasingly, art dealers are relying on events to contact clients; the presentation of fairs, exhibitions, or lectures is taking up more and more of their time. Pairing up with a cultural event, whether as a partner or simply by holding an exhibition at the same time, is a popular strategy. As always, scientific publications are a very good means to prove and convey one's substantial expertise. Also effective are the other services offered by dealerships, such as delivery, restoration, or the ability to take back mistaken purchases.

As for the auction houses, they too have a number of challenges in the sales sector. Admittedly, participating in an auction is a great experience, even for seasoned collectors. Experiences in recent years show that even in the age of the Internet, buyers still long for emotional ties to the objects they want to acquire. Therefore, the eventful nature of the auction is an added value that no dealer can match. The "magic of the auction," the battle for works of art, and attention-getting records comprise the auction house's great sales advantage.

However, it is not always possible to achieve record prices with high estimates; in the interest of sales, knowledgeable buyers demand modesty when it comes to estimates. Here, though, one factor—which usually fades into the background, because the main focus is on the private client—becomes obvious. Due to the rapid pace of sales and the more or less unique status of each object, the auction, as a distribution system, must always find new buyers for every offering!

New methods of finding clients, services (especially of the financial kind), and ties to the gallery system bring more private clients into the auction room, particularly in the top market segments, but they have also watered down the archaic auction process. In the middle market, though, methods for increasing consignments and sales are not particularly important; the lack of financial services or other expensive means of winning over clients actually contributes to the profitability of this market segment. Despite their professionalization, these auctions also prove that most of their clientele is regional or national, and therefore, the international auction houses' excursions into the middle market segments should only have a mild effect on national markets.

Experiments with "pure" Internet auctions have to be regarded as failures. The pleasure to be had at a live auction is one of the reasons to entertain reservations about the medium, and its doubtful security and remoteness are further reasons. Ultimately, the inability to reconcile the unique qualities of Internet business with the service, discretion, and especially quality of goods expected from the large auction houses caused projects in the top market segments to fail. The future lies in transmitting the live auction via the Internet.

A Review and Some Conclusions

Buying and Selling through Auctions and Trade

The question of whether to buy and sell through auction houses or dealers is subject to a number of determining factors. Clear-sighted consideration of the options will help clients reach a decision in their own personal case: the bottom line, however, is that the more valuable the object is, the better the auction will serve as a sales mechanism.

For the seller, the auction has several advantages. Since there is an asymmetrical distribution of information on the demand side, a loose estimate—like the ones offered by art dealers—contains the risk that the price is either too high and no buyers will be found, or else that it is lower than what a potential buyer might be prepared to pay for the piece. In an auction, however, prices are determined on the buyer's side. Hence, the seller can assume that the price realized represents the highest one that potential buyers are willing to pay. There are other advantages, as well: the seller does not have to wait until a buyer is found, but rather, determines the time of sale himself. If the seller consigns the job to a third party, then he is assured that the open bidding process will prevent a buyer forming a coalition with the intermediary. However, in order to take advantage of these things, the seller cannot be wary of the resulting publicity for his work of art; if that is the case, then the dealer is the more discreet alternative.

For the seller, the disadvantage of an auction is the higher cost associated with the sale. Unlike the dealer, who either directly buys a piece or takes it on commission, an auction sale not only entails a commission, but also the costs for catalogue illustrations, insurance, and shipping, regardless of whether or not the sale is successful. This demonstrates that there is a financial limit, below which it does not pay to sell an object at an auction, since the associated costs are simply too high in relation to the value of the piece.

In order to sell a work on the international market—that is, at auction in London, New York, Paris, or Hong Kong—demand must also be international. This can dissolve into thin air if a piece is no longer market fresh. In addition, this kind of auction is only worth the effort when a piece is so valuable that shipping and insurance costs will not eat up the majority of the profit.

An Inventory of Changes on the Market

Even though the art market in its current form still follows traditional rules and regulations, it has rarely gone through as many changes as it has since the turn of the twenty-first century. Auction houses have finally managed to develop from wholesalers into retailers. This has only been possible because, from the buyer's point of view, they have been able to establish themselves as a third form of distribution, alongside the art fairs and the gallery or trade system. The new buyers at auction are mainly private clients, who potentially spend more than commercial dealers, and are more open to methods of gaining and maintaining client contacts. Another big advantage for both sellers and the auction house is that private bidders prevent dealers from forming rings, or at least make it much more difficult for them to do so.

With respect to the objects and their characteristics, a variety of marketing instruments are used to find new clients. Of major importance here is the myth of the auction, which companies in all segments of the market strive to uphold, in order to make the supposedly burdensome purchase at auction seem more attractive. American clients are particularly susceptible to the allure of the auction room, and this has motivated all of the big auction houses to expand their

New York branches over the course of the last two decades, as they attempt to accommodate the larger audiences at live auctions.

Generally speaking, auction houses have greatly increased their public relations efforts, and these already determine the auction calendar and hence the selection of goods. In contrast, art dealers have reacted to the continuing fragmentation of the market mainly by specializing in niches.

Due to the focus on new ways to market objects, more emphasis has been placed on the characteristics that will distinguish a piece from others of its kind, or at least from similar objects: provenance and market freshness. On the basis of interesting provenances alone, auction houses are capable of generating entire market segments.

Establishing the auction as a form of distribution has made the boundaries between dealers and auction houses more permeable. With auction houses buying up or at least acquiring shares of galleries and art dealerships at all levels of the market, they are creating opaque alliances with the trade. Increasingly, private clients are reacting to this by turning to independent consultants.

The last gap between the auction house and the art dealer is being closed by the auction houses, which arrange private sales, when necessary. The auction houses' attempts to integrate the Internet auction as a rolling sale into their business models failed after a surprisingly brief period of time; obviously, the chance to see the original object in person is an indispensible element in the high-end segment of the market. In addition, it is expected that there will be increasing desire for direct experiences with art in the still young, "virtual" century. The future lies in transmitting the live auction via the Internet.

Only art fairs continue to exclude auction companies and thus avoid the above-mentioned coexistence of the dealer and auction systems. Art fairs are a very important way for dealers to celebrate their profession in a large-scale event. It is yet to be seen if the art fairs can continue to exclude the auction houses, or if the Asian model will be adopted in the future—so that auction houses will come to produce art fairs, and galleries will hold auctions.

Aside from the convergence of the two distribution systems, the boundaries of the art market have also been blurred elsewhere, especially between the commercial and non-commercial sectors, owing to the financial difficulties of the museums. However, the art market has so far avoided dovetailing with the international luxury goods industry. Attempts to turn international auction houses in particular into "art boutiques" affiliated with fashion companies, and thus to have access to their clientele, have not been successful. As a result, auction houses are left with even higher expenditures for finding new clients, and a strong awareness of the value of the brand as part of the corporate identity of their own companies.

As far as the individual markets are concerned, it is clear that the objects in the most upscale, highest segments of the market sell in New York and in Europe. London has maintained its leading role in the areas of applied arts and the Old Masters. Paris has compensated for the loss of the contemporary art market to New York by concentrating on Impressionism and the applied arts. London benefits from the fact that "new" buyers from Asia and the former Soviet Union prefer London to New York. The European market also profits from the fact that the art market is so far surprisingly unaffected by any European harmonization of inheritance or tax laws.

Clearly, it is becoming more difficult for dealers to thrive in the face of competition from international auction houses. In the last decade, the only successful art fairs were those at the very top and bottom of the market, and this reflects the development of the market as a whole, in miniature. Dealers, however, will continue to be the more discreet sales channel, and thus, they will gradually become less dependent on market trends. As always, the dealer's best chances lie in his expertise, his specialization, his ability to offer a variety of services, and in the trust between himself and his clientele.

Future Directions and Conclusion

Auction houses and dealers exist in symbiosis. Without dealer consignments, no house could hold auctions, and without items bought at auction, dealers would have difficulties filling their showrooms. In fields where this symbiosis is not yet particularly advanced, it will develop accordingly. Auction houses have long been familiar with the artist's studio as a supply source, and galleries, which until now have bought exclusively from their own artists and have been afraid of artists selling their work directly at auction, will eventually buy their works at an auction, if they are available at attractive prices. This might impair the core business of a gallery, but it will not eliminate the profession per se, because thanks primarily to the work of galleries, the art market can retain its role as a trend scout, which makes it a part of art history. Even though the luxury goods industry has been preparing since the nineteen-nineties to take over this part, a work of art still has an advantage over an industrially made luxury product: its uniqueness, its aura.

On the market, the distinction between masterpieces and filler will be stronger. Over the long term, anyone who stimulates the market with outstanding artworks will succeed. This will also affect the various sales channels. To the extent that middle market goods remain unsold, most dealers and auction houses will have to choose a segment—the generalist is dying out. Even the most aggressive expansion of an auction house cannot hide the fact that it is not capable of serving every segment of the market. Thus, dealers will find it easier to survive in fields where it does not pay to hold an auction, primarily because the seller's associated costs are too high. At the same time, the dealer at the other end of the quality scale can take advantage of the fact that auction houses will have to withdraw from shrinking market segments, since a critical mass of items is needed to put together an auction. Traditionally, the market's extremely large base has not been very profitable; only a few, well-established, financially sound dealers or consortiums will be able to survive in shrinking market segments. The question posed at the beginning of this book—whether or not the expansion of auction houses actually has the potential to force art dealers to the edges of the art market—may be answered hesitantly, yet definitely, in the affirmative.

Selected Literature

Akinsha, Konstantin, and Grigorii **Kozlov**. *Beautiful Loot: The Soviet Plunder of Europe's Art Treasures.* New York, 1995.

Alsop, Joseph. *The Rare Art Traditions: The History of Art Collecting and Its Linked Phenomena Wherever These Have Appeared.* London, 1982.

Artale, Angelo. *Rings in Auctions: An Experimental Approach.* Berlin, Heidelberg, and New York, 1997.

Ashenfelter, Orley, and Kathryn **Graddy**. *Art Auctions: A Survey of Empirical Studies.* Cambridge, Massachusetts, 2002.

Assouline, Pierre. *An Artful Life.* New York, 1991.

Barron, Stephanie, ed. *"Degenerate Art": The Fate of the Avant-Garde in Nazi Germany.* Los Angeles, 1991.

Behrmann, Siegfried. *Duveen.* Vienna, 1953.

Benjamin, Walter. *The Work of Art in the Age of Mechanical Reproduction.* First published in German in 1936.

Bennigsen, Silvia von, Irene **Gludowacz**, and Susanne van **Hagen**. *Global Art.* Ostfildern, 2009.

Berggruen, Heinz. *Hauptweg und Nebenwege.* Berlin, 1996.

Bonus, Holger, and Dieter **Ronte**. *Credibility and Economic Value in the Visual Arts.* Münster, 1995.

Bourdieu, Pierre. *Distinction: A Social Critique of the Judgement of Taste.* London, 1984

Byrne-Sutton, Quentin, and Fabienne **Geisinger-Mariethoz**. *Art-Law Guide.* Geneva, 1999.

Cassady, Ralph. *Auctions and Auctioneering.* Berkeley, 1967.

Collings, Matthew. *Art Crazy Nation.* London, 2001.

Collings, Matthew. *Blimey!* London, 1997.

Cox, Donald, ed. *Risk Taking and Information Handling in Consumer Behavior.* Boston, 1967.

Duveen, Joseph. *The Rise of the House of Duveen.* London, 1957.

Engelbrecht-Wiggans, Richard. *Auctions, Bidding, and Contracting.* New York, 1983.

Felix, Zdenek, Beate **Hentschel**, and Dirk **Luckow**, eds. *Art & Economy.* Hamburg, 2002.

Feliciano, Hector. *The Lost Museum.* New York, 1997.

Flick, Gert-Rudolf. *Missing Masterpieces: Lost Works of Art 1450–1900.* London, 2003.

Freeland, Cynthia. *Art Theory.* New York, 2001.

Frey, Bruno. *Arts & Economics: Analysis & Cultural Policy.* Heidelberg, 2000.

Frey, Bruno, and Werner **Pommerehne**. *Muses and Markets: Explorations in the Economics of the Arts.* Cambridge, Massachusetts, 1989.

Gaillard, Yann, Alain **Quemin**, Philippe **Chalmin**, Christian **Borel**, Gerard **Sousi**, and Laurence **Mauger**. *Code des ventes volontaires et judiciaires.* Lyon, 2001.

Galenson, David W. *The Life-Cycles of Modern Artists.* New York, 2002.

Goethe, Johann Wolfgang von. *Der Sammler und die Seinigen.* Dresden, 1997.

Guggenheim, Peggy. *Confessions of an Art Addict.* Hopewell, New Jersey, 1997.

Guilbaut, Serge. *How New York Stole the Idea of Modern Art.* Chicago, 1985.

Herbert, John. *Inside Christie's.* New York, 1990.

Herrmann, Frank. *Sotheby's: Portrait of an Auction House.* London, 1980.

Hertz, Richard, ed. *Theories of Contemporary Art.* Englewood Cliffs, New Jersey, 1985.

Hogrefe, Jeffrey. *Wholly Unacceptable: The Bitter Battle for Sotheby's.* New York, 1986.

Hörmann, Ingeborg. *The Vernissage.* London, 1991.

Huiberts, Ard, and Sander **Kooistra**. *Valse Kunst.* Amsterdam, 2003.

Kabakov, Ilya. *On the "Total" Installation.* Ostfildern-Ruit, 1995.

Klein, Naomi. *No Logo!* New York, 2000.

Lacey, Robert. *Sotheby's: Bidding for Class.* Boston, 1998.

Learmount, Brian. *A History of the Auction.* London, 1985.

Muensterberger, Werner. *Collecting: An Unruly Passion.* San Diego, New York, and London, 1994.

Nicholas, Lynn. *The Rape of Europa: The Fate of Europe's Treasures in the Third Reich and the Second World War.* New York, 1994.

Norton, Thomas. *100 Years of Collecting in America: The Story of Sotheby ParkeBernet.* New York, 1984.

Panofsky, Erwin. *Idea: Ein Beitrag zur Begriffsgeschichte der älteren Kunsttheorie.* Berlin, 1993.

Petropoulos, Jonathan. *The Faustian Bargain: The Art World in Nazy Germany.* Oxford, 2000.

Powell, Nicholas. *Christie's.* Paris, 1999.

Saltzman, Cynthia. *The Portrait of Dr. Gachet—The Story of a Van Gogh Masterpiece: Money, Politics, Collectors, Greed, and Loss.* New York, 1998.

Shapton, Leanne. *Important Artifacts and Personal Property from the Collection of Lenore Doolan and Harrold Morris, including Books, Street Fashion and Jewelry.* New York, 2009.

Smith, Charles. *Auctions: The Social Construction of Value.* London, 1989.

Stechl, Margarethe. *Auction Houses in the Fine Art Market.* Vienna, 1995.

Thompson, Don. *The $12 Million Stuffed Shark.* London, 2008.

Tomkins, Calvin. *Merchants & Masterpieces.* New York, 1989.

Watson, Peter. *From Monet to Manhattan: The Rise of the Modern Art Market.* New York, 1992.

Watson, Peter. *Sotheby's: Inside Story.* London, 1997.

Wechsler, Helen, Teri **Coate-Saal**, and John **Lukavic**. *Museum Policy and Procedures for Nazi-Era Issues.* Washington, D.C., 2001.

Wildenstein, Daniel, and Yves **Stavrides**. *Marchands d'art.* Paris, 1999.

Wilhelm, Henry, and Carol **Brower**. *The Permanence and Care of Color Photographs.* Grinnell, Iowa, 1993.

Williams, Robert. *Russian Art and American Money 1900–1940.* Cambridge, 1980.

Wood, Christopher. *The Great Art Boom 1970–1997.* London, 1997.

Name Index

Index

Dirk Boll

Managing Director, Christie's Zurich
European Director, Christie's International

Dirk Boll, born in 1970 in Kassel, studied law at the universities of Göttingen and Freiburg am Breisgau. He practiced law in Stuttgart and Brussels before doing graduate studies in cultural management, which ultimately led him to the art market. He began his career at Christie's in London in 1998. After a stint as the company's representative in Germany and head of the Stuttgart office, he transferred to Zurich in late 2004 and since then has been stationed there as both Managing Director and European Director.

Boll has taught cultural management in Hamburg since 2001, and began teaching the same subject in Zurich in 2011. His articles on current art market developments are published regularly in international magazines and daily newspapers, and he writes a weekly column on the art market for the Swiss financial magazine, *Stocks,* published by Springer Media.

Translations Allison Plath-Moseley

Copyediting Anne O'Connor

Graphic design and typesetting Gabriele Sabolewski, Hatje Cantz

Typeface FF Din, Melior

Production Christine Emter, Hatje Cantz

Paper EuroBulk, 135 g/m²

Printing and binding CPI books GmbH, Leck

Published by
Hatje Cantz Verlag
Zeppelinstrasse 32
73760 Ostfildern
Germany
Tel. +49 711 4405-200
Fax +49 711 4405-220
www.hatjecantz.com

Hatje Cantz books are available internationally at selected bookstores. For more information about our distribution partners, please visit our website at www.hatjecantz.com.

ISBN 978-3-7757-2815-7 (English)
ISBN 978-3-7757-2814-0 (German)

This book is also available as an e-book
ISBN 978-3-7757-3009-9 (English)
ISBN 978-3-7757-3008-2 (German)

Printed in Germany

Acknowledgments
BSV, Alexander Farenholtz, Felix Ghezzi, Susanne Meyer-Abich, Anne Rüffer, Stephanie Tasch